WHERE TO TAKE THE KIDS INDIANAPOLIS

PLAYGROUNDS, CULTURE, NATURE, AND FUN

Katy Mann

REEDY PRESS

Dedication

To my babies, Lucy, Scout, Shaundi, James, and Quinn, may you always see the world through a lens of joy. This book is a love letter to you and to the city we call home. And to Jacob, my partner in everything, thank you for helping make this life so full of magic, laughter, and love.

Reedy Press
PO Box 5131
St. Louis, MO 63139
reedypress.com

Library of Congress Control Number: 2025944307

ISBN: 9781681066011

Printed in the United States of America
25 26 27 28 29   5 4 3 2 1

Acknowledgments

So many wonderful people have played a role in my success and helped make this project possible. Thank you again to the talented team at Indy with Kids. I'm especially grateful for the time, wisdom, friendship, and shared experiences of Tori Kincaid, Lisa Viaches, Sara Keller, Stephanie Greenwald, Ashley Dykton, Jessica Deubner, Dannielle Messoroch, and so many others who've been part of this journey.

Mom and Dad, thank you for giving me life and for your unwavering support. I love you.

Jim and Carol, Mike and Sharon: thank you for being my Indiana family. I love you, too.

There's something special about the Indianapolis community that makes it feel like home. Thank you for embracing my family, my work, and me with so much kindness.

To our church family: thank you for years of encouragement, whether in seasons of celebration or challenge.

To the incredible moms and dads who make up our village: you've fed, clothed, and chauffeured my children. You've cheered them on from the sidelines and answered my SOS texts without hesitation. Thank you to my fellow school/baseball/show-choir/softball/soccer/art/theater/cheer/flag-football parents.

And of course, much love to my MAJK moms, Michelle, Ann-Marie, and Jenny.

A big thank you to the crew at Reedy Press for your hard work, and to Faith Blackwell for the headshots.

Table of Contents

Introduction

There's something truly special about raising kids in Central Indiana, but you already know that. Maybe it's the way people work hard to make this the best place to be or how a spontaneous trip to a museum, park, or festival is always just around the corner. It's a region where families can enjoy the best of both worlds: access to both big-city attractions and small towns and farming communities.

This book is your guide to exploring all the family-friendly and kid-approved adventures that Indianapolis and the surrounding communities have to offer. From world-class destinations like The Children's Museum of Indianapolis and the Indianapolis Zoo to local gems tucked away in small towns, you'll find ideas for every season, every age, and every kind of family. If you're in search of a rainy-day play space, a quick weekend outing, or a hidden trail perfect for wandering, it's all here.

In Indianapolis, childhood is a magical stage, parenthood is a time you'll never forget, and this book will help you make the most of every moment.

Best Place for Fearless Adventurers

KOTEEWI RANGE

11909 Koteewi Dr., Noblesville
(317) 776-8472
koteewiarchery.com

If your family loves adventure, you'll want to check out Strawtown Koteewi Park. This 800-acre historic park is packed with outdoor experiences, from horseback riding and aerial obstacle courses to winter snow tubing and more.

At Koteewi Range, archery is a hit with all ages. With 96 lanes for every skill level, you can take aim at Olympic-style targets or add some fun with 3D animal figures. Kids especially enjoy pretending they're heroes from their favorite movies or storybooks. All equipment is provided, but you're welcome to bring your own gear if you'd like.

NICKEL PLATE EXPRESS RAILBIKE EXCURSIONS

825 Forest Park Dr., Noblesville
nickelplateexpress.com

Nickel Plate Express offers railbikes: pedal-powered vehicles that seat up to four passengers. These family-friendly rides are a unique and leisurely way to explore the scenic Indiana countryside, with multiple excursion lengths available along the historic Nickel Plate railroad tracks.

Try the Forest Park Rail Adventure, a seven-mile round-trip journey through lush woodlands and picturesque farmland. For a shorter option, the White River Family Cruise is a quick ride across the White River, with a stop in downtown Noblesville to explore local shops and eateries. For a memorable evening, pedal into the sunset on the Twilight Rail Ride and enjoy s'mores by the fire at the turnaround point.

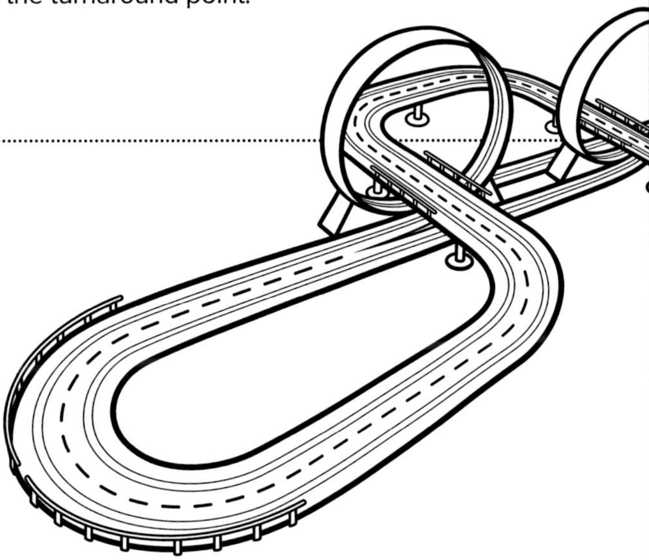

INDY RC RACEWAY & HOBBIES

5135 S Emerson Ave.,
Indianapolis
(317) 787-7568
indyrcraceway.net

Tucked inside a hobby shop, Indy RC Raceway is a hidden gem for families who love fast-paced fun on a smaller scale. Whether you want to join the race or simply watch, this 7,000-square-foot indoor track is full of nonstop action.

RC cars and trucks of all kinds take turns tearing around the track, so there's always something cool happening. Spectators are welcome, and watching the tiny vehicles zip by is surprisingly exciting.

If your kids (or you!) get hooked, the hobby shop is stocked with RC cars, trucks, and gear, and the friendly staff is happy to help you find your first ride.

Best Place for High-Flying Fun

SOLDIERS & SAILORS MONUMENT

1 Monument Cir., Indianapolis
(317) 232-7615
in.gov/iwm

Standing 284 feet, 6 inches tall, the Soldiers & Sailors Monument honors Hoosier veterans from conflicts including the Revolutionary War, War of 1812, and Civil War. Climbing to the top is a rite of passage for local kids, and best of all, it's free. You can climb all 330 steps to the observation deck or take the elevator most of the way, leaving just 49 steps to reach the top, where glass windows reveal one-of-a-kind views of Indianapolis.

Strollers aren't allowed inside the tower, and there are no public restrooms on-site. Neither the stairwell nor the elevator is climate-controlled, so on hot days, access may be limited for safety.

GO APE ZIPLINE AND ADVENTURE PARK

5855 Delong Rd., Indianapolis
(800) 971-8271
goape.com

The Go Ape Treetop Adventure is great for thrill-seekers ages 10 and up who are at least four feet, seven inches tall. With 40 obstacles suspended up to 41 feet in the air, this self-guided experience is ideal for adventurous kids. Zip lines, climbing ropes, suspended bridges, and tree trunk ladders challenge participants as they make their way from tree to tree. The most daring kids won't want to miss the free-drop Tarzan swing.

A safety briefing kicks things off; you'll be fitted with a harness and shown the ropes by trained staff. Kids 15 and under must be accompanied by a participating adult (one adult per two children). Gloves are recommended, and all other equipment is provided.

Younger children can give the Forest EscAPE a try. This outdoor escape room-style activity is great for ages 5 and up with their adults. Families have one hour to complete the challenge in the woods.

KOTEEWI AERIAL ADVENTURE PARK AND TREETOP TRAILS

11800 Koteewi Dr., Noblesville
(800) 590-8347
koteewiadventures.com

Koteewi Aerial Adventure Park, located within Strawtown Koteewi Park, was created for those seeking adventure off the ground. There are zip lines, rope bridges, and climbing elements high in the treetops. Kids ages 7-9 can join in with a participating adult, those who are 10-13 may join with adult supervision, and ages 14 and up can navigate the courses independently. These adventures last about two and a half hours and should be booked in advance.

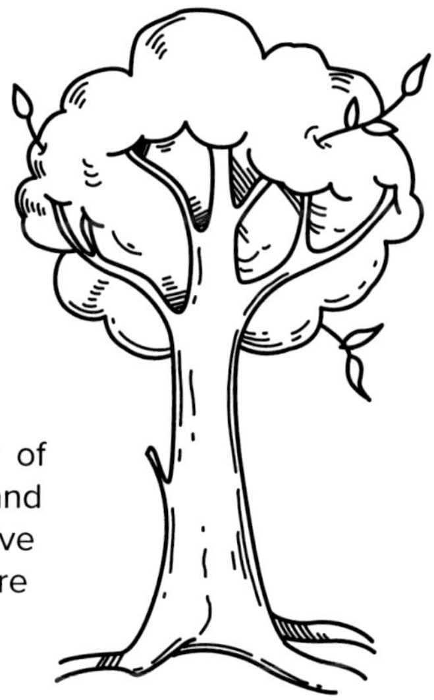

While you're there, stop by the Taylor Center of Natural History and archaeological site. Kids and adults can view real artifacts and learn about Native American communities that lived in the area more than 700 years ago.

Best Place to Practice Acrobatics

CIRQUE INDY

617 N Fulton St., Indianapolis
(317) 758-7455
cirqueindy.com

Cirque Indy is an aerial and circus arts studio where kids can take classes in silks, trapeze, aerial hoops (lyra), and acrobatics, just like what they'd see in a real circus show. It's a fantastic way to build strength, coordination, and confidence through movement.

The best part? There's no need to buy any special equipment; just wear comfy clothes and show up ready to fly. Instead of climbing on furniture at home, kids can safely swing, flip, and hang with expert instruction.

Try an affordable taster class to see if it's a fit, or host a birthday party with a circus twist.

COLTS CANAL PLAYSPACE

701 Canal Walk, Indianapolis

Colts Canal Playspace is a must-visit downtown Indy destination where kids can run, climb, and explore right along the Canal. Built in partnership with the Indianapolis Colts, this urban playground isn't like typical playgrounds; it has giant climbing nets, slides, and obstacle-course-style play equipment.

It's especially great if you have older kids looking for something beyond the usual swings and monkey bars. Every part of the space invites climbing, jumping, and active play. Don't worry, your younger ones will love it too.

The park's location is perfect for people-watching, relaxing by the water, or taking a break after paddle boating or visiting nearby attractions. It's free, fun, and perfectly placed for a downtown adventure.

FUNTIME AT WRIGHT'S GYMNASTICS

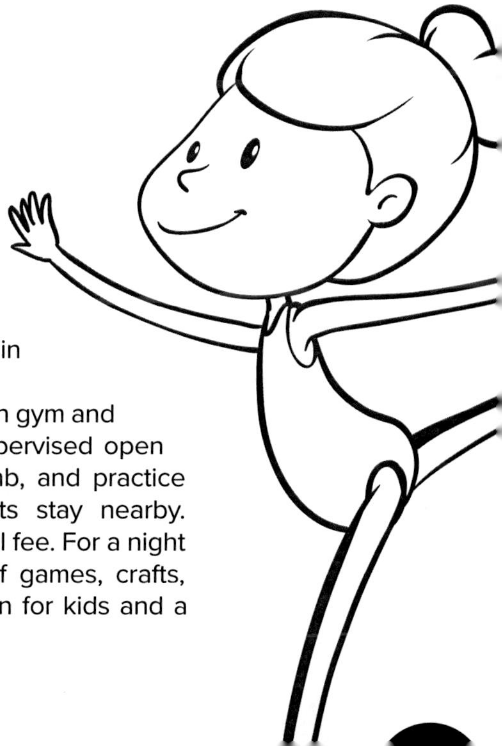

Center Grove, Greenwood,
Fishers, Noblesville, Westfield
wrightsgymnastics.com

Wright's Gymnastics offers dance, gymnastics, and NinjaZone classes across its six Central Indiana locations. Kids build strength, learn cool new skills, and have tons of fun in every class.

Wright's is also home to FUNtime open gym and Kids' Night Out events. FUNtime is supervised open play where kids can jump, swing, climb, and practice tricks in the giant gym while parents stay nearby. FUNtime is open to the public for a small fee. For a night off, try Kids' Night Out: three hours of games, crafts, activities, and dinner included. It's a win for kids and a break for parents.

Best Place for Laser Tag Battles

LASER FLASH

617 Third Ave. SW, Carmel
(317) 571-1677
laser-flash.com

Laser tag is a fast-paced game where players race through a dark, glow-in-the-dark arena, tagging opponents with infrared laser blasters while dodging incoming beams.

Laser Flash is Indiana's largest laser tag arena, featuring a multi-level glow-in-the-dark battlefield filled with ramps, obstacles, and hiding spots. Players ages 7 and up can participate in 15-minute games that keep everyone moving and strategizing. This is a dedicated space built entirely for laser tag fun, and it is a favorite among laser tag fanatics.

When you're not in the arena, head to the arcade for more fun between rounds. The Laser Flash snack bar offers pizza, drinks, and other kid-friendly treats to refuel after the game.

COMBAT OPS

4650 E Southport Rd., Indianapolis
(888) 528-7775
combatops.com

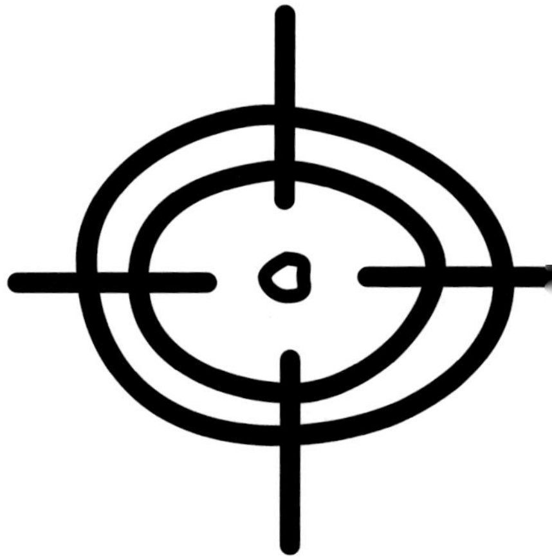

Combat Ops is more than just laser tag—it's a full-blown entertainment center packed with tons of exciting activities. The military-themed laser tag arena makes kids feel like they're on a real mission, with glowing lights, obstacles, and plenty of places to duck and hide.

If your child loves Nerf battles, they'll enjoy the action in a soft, padded turf arena. Combat Ops also features mini golf, virtual reality, a laser maze, dodgeball, an arcade, and axe throwing. With no official age limit, participation is at parents' discretion, perfect for families with kids of different ages. There's always something new and exciting being added to the lineup.

BOWL 32

845 Westfield Rd., Noblesville
(317) 773-3381
bowl32.com

Bowl 32 offers one of the most affordable laser tag experiences around. Each game is just $5 per player. The blacklight, two-level arena is full of twists, turns, and hiding spots, perfect for kids ages 5 and up (as long as the vest fits securely on their shoulders). Games last about 7.5 minutes, with new rounds starting every 15 minutes.

While you wait for your next mission to begin, check out the arcade, axe throwing, glow-in-the-dark mini golf, or bowling; the snack bar serves up food and drinks. It's a great place for families to play, celebrate, and compete.

Best Climbing Spot to Hang Tight

CLIMB TIME INDY

8750 Corporation Dr., Indianapolis
(317) 596-3335
climbtimeindy.com

This indoor rock climbing gym has multiple walls and routes for all skill levels, so whether your kids are just starting out or already love to climb, there's a challenge waiting for them. From beginner-friendly walls to more advanced routes that test strength and problem-solving skills, your whole family will have a great time.

Even first-timers will feel comfortable, thanks to the welcoming staff who help with harnesses, clipping in, and climbing safety. Once everyone gets the hang of it, you'll be racing to the top together. If your kids enjoy climbing, Climb Time also offers classes and memberships, including options for families.

NORTH MASS BOULDER

1411 Roosevelt Ave., Indianapolis
(317) 953-6667
northmassboulder.com

If you're searching for an exciting and active experience for your kids, introduce them to climbing at North Mass Boulder, the largest climbing gym in Indiana. The facility features a wide range of climbing terrain suitable for all skill levels, along with dedicated youth climbing areas.

Climbing shoes are available for rent, and first-time guests receive complimentary shoe rentals. Children must be supervised throughout the visit, so it's a great activity to try together as a family. North Mass Boulder also has a robust social calendar with events, camps, and competitions. You can even host a children's birthday party on-site. While you're visiting, enjoy a meal or snack at the Top Out Café.

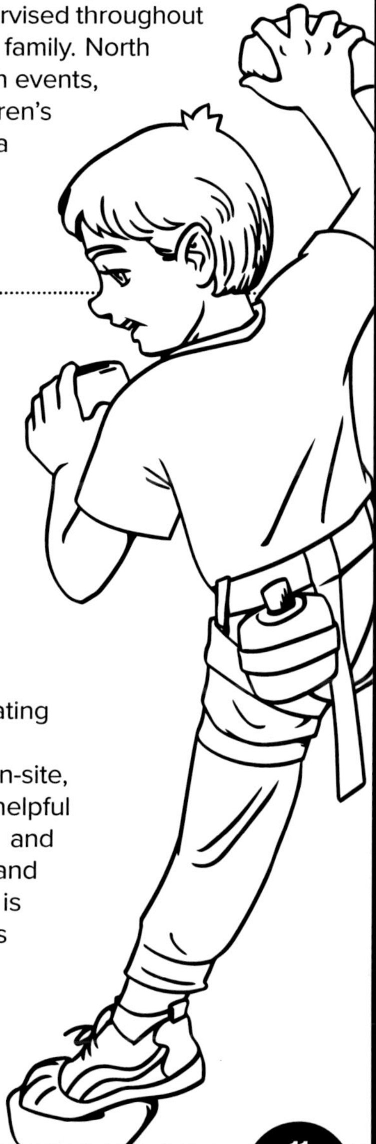

HOOSIER HEIGHTS

9850 Mayflower Park Dr., Carmel
(317) 802-9302
hoosierheightsindianapolis.com

Hoosier Heights indoor climbing gym offers an array of climbing challenges perfect for beginners, including auto belays that enable kids to explore the vertical walls with ease. For more experienced climbers, the gym features rotating routes that offer a fresh challenge each visit.

Families can rent climbing shoes and harnesses on-site, and the friendly staff provides instruction and a helpful orientation to ensure everyone feels confident and secure before getting started. Children 5 years and under climb free, and climbing gear rental is complimentary on your first visit. The day pass is great for families; you're welcome to leave for lunch or a nap and return later the same day.

Best Place to Introduce Kids to Art

FIRST FRIDAY

Various locations
indyarts.org

First Fridays are like a giant art party that happens on the first Friday of every month. It's a night when artists show off their newest paintings, sculptures, murals, and other creative works. You can walk through galleries, watch live painting, and often join in on opportunities to make some art yourself.

There's usually live music, so you might hear a cool band or catch a street performance. Some spots even have dancers, DJs, and fun light displays. If you get hungry, there are food trucks serving up delicious snacks like pizza, tacos, and sweet treats, and some galleries offer complimentary snacks and beverages.

Most galleries are family-friendly. Our favorites include the Harrison Center, the Fountain Square neighborhood, the Tube Factory Artspace, and the Factory Arts District.

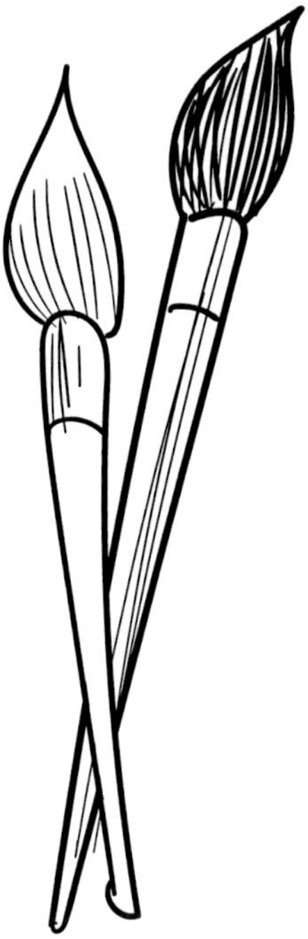

INDIANAPOLIS ART CENTER

820 E 67th St., Indianapolis
(317) 255-2464
indyartcenter.org

A visit to the Indianapolis Art Center is a great way to spark creativity and see amazing art. It's not just a museum. Yes, there's fantastic artwork to admire, but visitors can also create their own masterpieces through classes and workshops. Try your hand at painting, pottery, drawing, or even glassblowing. There are even classes and summer camps specifically for kids.

The most popular space is the outdoor art park. Sculptures and expressions of creativity are tucked throughout the natural setting. Head out on the trails and see what you discover. Some pieces are interactive, giving kids a chance to engage with the art in playful ways. Snap photos, sit by the river, or just soak up some creative inspiration.

WORLD'S SMALLEST CHILDREN'S ART GALLERY

40 W Main St., Carmel
carmelartscouncil.org/childrens-gallery

For a bite-sized art excursion, visit this tiny gallery showcasing artwork created by kids. Snuggled into Carmel's Arts & Design District, the World's Smallest Children's Art Gallery is a one-room space with rotating exhibits of local children's artwork, and it holds a world record! In 1999, it was certified by Guinness World Records as the smallest children's art gallery in the world.

Hours and exhibits vary, but it's worth stopping by for aspiring young artists or world-record chasers. Afterward, explore the Arts & Design District; grab a treat from a nearby bakery, browse the boutiques, or check out the "Man on the Street" sculptures by J. Seward Johnson Jr.

Best Place for Arts and Crafts

PENN & BEECH CANDLE COMPANY

145 Elm St., Carmel
(317) 689-0789

8698 E 116th St., Fishers
(317) 218-7574

747 N College Ave., Indianapolis
(317) 721-6885
pennandbeech.com

Step into a studio filled with over 100 amazing aromas, from freshly cut grass to Honeycrisp apple. At Penn & Beech Candle Company, the whole family can create their very own candles or collaborate on a group candle. First, you'll explore all the fragrance options and pick your favorites. Then, with help from the friendly staff, you'll mix your custom scent and blend it with hot wax.

Once you've poured your unique creation into the jar of your choice, you'll leave it to set and come back later to pick it up. This activity is especially great for older kids, though younger ones can join in with a little help. Expect to spend about an hour crafting your aromatic masterpiece.

KICASSO SNEAKER ART BAR

6416 Ferguson St., Indianapolis
(317) 500-7332
kicassoindy.com

Don't wear plain old tennis shoes; turn those kicks into custom art at Kicasso Sneaker Art Bar. This one-of-a-kind studio lets you design and paint your own sneakers. Bring your own leather or canvas pair, or book a class that includes canvas sneakers or even Converse.

Once you're checked in, grab some paint and start creating. The friendly staff is full of tips and techniques to help your shoes look amazing, even if you're not a pro. There are tons of colors, stencils, and design ideas to spark your imagination. You're also welcome to bring your own snacks and drinks. Plan to spend about two hours making your masterpiece.

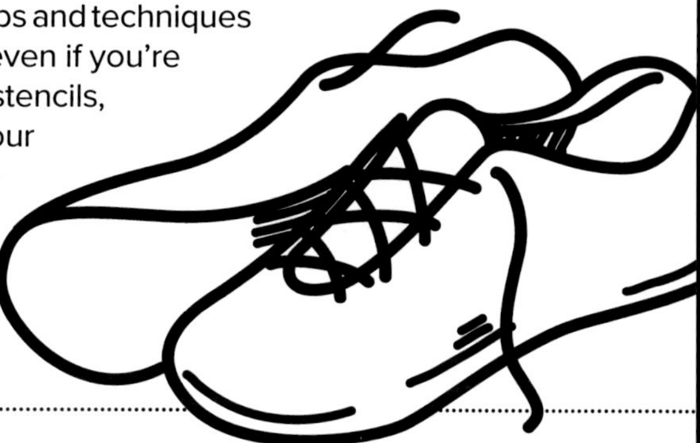

TIE DYE LAB

7508 Beechwood Centre Rd. #500, Avon
(317) 742-7008
thetiedyelab.com

For kids who love getting creative and making cool wearable art, the Tie Dye Lab in Avon is the place to be. It's a DIY tie-dye studio where you can design your own shirts, socks, pillowcases, and more.

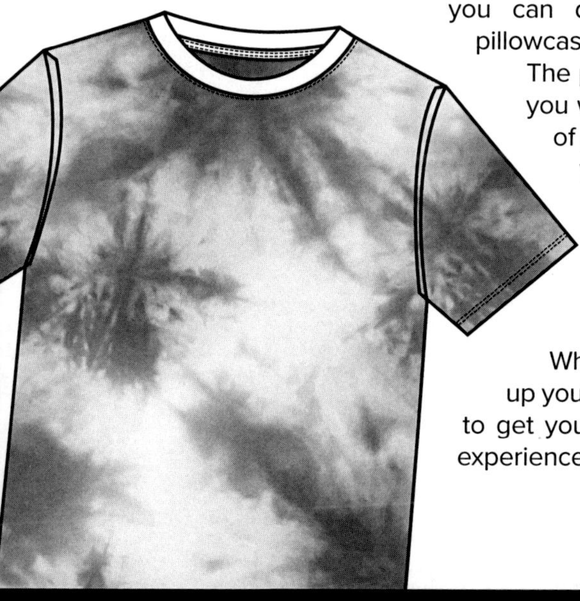

The process is super simple: pick what you want to tie-dye from the collection of garments and accessories, choose your favorite color combinations, and use fun techniques to make your one-of-a-kind design. The best part? No cleanup! The staff takes care of all the messy stuff, so you just get to enjoy the fun. When you're done, they'll package up your creation with instructions on how to get your item ready to wear. The whole experience takes just under an hour.

Best Spot for Creative Kids

KURT VONNEGUT MUSEUM & LIBRARY

543 Indiana Ave., Indianapolis
(317) 423-0391
vonnegutlibrary.org

At the Kurt Vonnegut Museum & Library, you and your kids can explore the life and works of one of Indianapolis's most famous authors. The exhibits include Vonnegut's personal items, like his typewriter and Purple Heart medal, along with interactive displays.

You'll learn not just about Vonnegut's writing but also about causes he cared deeply about: free speech, banned books, and jailed authors. It's an outing with a mix of literature, art, and history. A visit here offers a unique perspective of Indianapolis and is sure to spark some inspired conversations with your young readers.

BRIGHTLY ART STUDIO

22 E Main St., Brownsburg
(317) 939-2947
brightlyartstudio.com

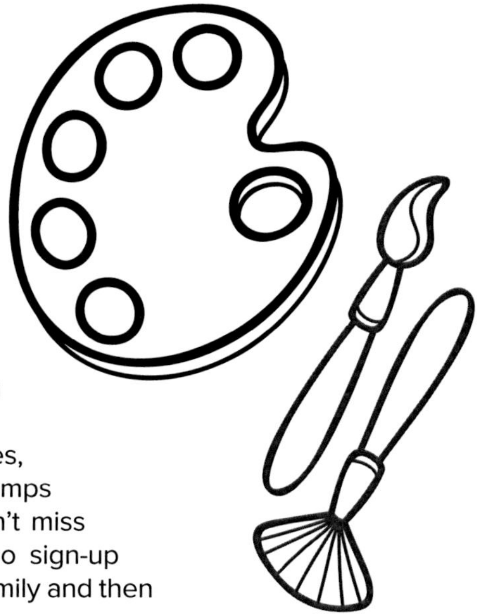

Whether your kids love painting, drawing, or crafting, Brightly Art Studio is a cheerful and inspiring place to let their creativity shine. The bright and multichromatic decor will grab their attention the moment they walk through the door.

Brightly offers all kinds of art experiences, from age-specific clubs and classes to camps and birthday parties. On weekends, don't miss Craft Café, an open studio time with no sign-up required. Just pay a studio fee for your family and then pick your favorite projects to make.

If you're looking to stock up on art supplies or find a creative gift, the Brightly Shop is filled with multichromatic inspiration.

ARTS FOR ALL PROGRAM

Select Indy Parks & Recreation locations
parks.indy.gov

The Arts for All program through Indy Parks & Recreation provides kids with a free, hands-on art activity right in their neighborhood, making art and creativity accessible to everyone. It's designed for ages 5 to 12, but anyone is welcome to join in the fun. All art supplies are provided for this drop-in activity, and you'll get to take your masterpiece home when you're done.

This weekly program runs for one hour at select Indy Parks locations. Each park hosts Arts for All on different dates and times, so be sure to check the schedule. The projects change every week, so there's always something new to create.

Best Hub for Page-Turning Stories

INDIANA YOUNG READERS CENTER

315 W Ohio St., Indianapolis
(317) 232-3719
in.gov/library/iyrc

Tucked inside the Indiana State Library is a hidden gem just for kids, the Indiana Young Readers Center. While the library holds a massive archive of Indiana's history through records, files, and books, this special space is dedicated to Hoosier authors and illustrators who write for children and teens.

You can explore a wonderful collection of children's and young adult books, enjoy story times, and check out special programs. Kids love picking out a book and settling into a cozy nook to read. Your youngest literature fans will adore the playhouse inspired by Indiana native Norman Bridwell's Clifford the Big Red Dog. Admission is free; check the website for current hours and events.

FABLES AND FAIRY TALES

38 N Main St., Martinsville
(765) 913-4100
fablesandfairytale.com

There's a charming bookstore just south of Indy, nestled right on the downtown Martinsville town square. Step inside Fables and Fairy Tales and you'll find shelves full of books for the whole family. The children's section is perfectly curated with timeless treasures and the latest hits, and the young adult section gets rave reviews from readers.

You'll also find classic toys, board games, and book-themed clothing, perfect for picking out a reward, gift, or surprise for your reading sidekick. The staff is fantastic at recommending books you didn't know you needed. Want the magic to continue? Sign up for a book subscription box and get a monthly surprise tailored just for you.

INDY READS

1066 Virginia Ave., Indianapolis
(317) 384-1496
indyreads.org

Indy Reads is an independent bookstore with a big heart and an even bigger mission: to build literacy, English language, and job readiness skills that empower adults and families. When you shop here, you're supporting that mission, because every purchase goes directly toward Indy Reads programming.

The shop is cozy, colorful, and packed with a mix of new and used books for all ages. There's always something happening too, with a calendar full of family-friendly events like chess club, story hour with performers, and author visits. It's the perfect place to curl up with a good book and be part of something meaningful.

Best Way to Celebrate Global Cultures and Traditions

GLOBAL VILLAGE WELCOME CENTER

4233 Lafayette Rd., Indianapolis
(317) 751-5229
imcoalition.org

The Global Village Welcome Center offers families a fun and immersive way to explore cultures from around the world. Through beautifully curated galleries, you can learn about the traditions and histories of Africa, Asia, Europe, the Americas, and beyond, through more than 5,000 artifacts on display.

Throughout the year, the Global Village hosts cultural celebrations like the Lunar New Year, Juneteenth, and the Holiday Bazaar & World of Trees. These events let you experience global traditions through music, dance, food, and hands-on workshops.

Looking for something fun and meaningful over summer break? Check out their themed camps and workshops for kids and teens.

DÍA DE MUERTOS COMMUNITY CELEBRATION & INDIAN MARKET AND FESTIVAL

The Eiteljorg Museum of American Indians and Western Art
500 W Washington St., Indianapolis
(317) 636-9378
eiteljorg.org

The Eiteljorg Museum hosts two unforgettable cultural celebrations each year that families absolutely love—the Día de Muertos Community Celebration and the Indian Market and Festival.

Every October, the Día de Muertos event honors loved ones who've passed with vibrant traditions from Mexico. The museum comes alive with dance performances, hands-on art-making, live music, and food. Don't miss the Community Art and Altar Exhibit, where you'll see stunning ofrendas (altars) created by local groups.

In June, the Indian Market and Festival brings together over 140 Native American artists from the US and Canada. Shop for jewelry, pottery, and paintings; try fry bread; and enjoy dancing, drumming, storytelling, and kid-friendly art activities.

MADAM WALKER LEGACY CENTER

617 Indiana Ave., Indianapolis
(317) 236-2099
madamwalkerlegacycenter.com

The Madam Walker Legacy Center honors the life of America's first self-made female millionaire, Madam C. J. Walker. She built a successful beauty empire creating hair care products for Black women and helped countless others through her work. Today, the center is a cultural hub and historic theater where you can learn her story and attend performances. The building itself is a National Historic Landmark, and you'll get to step inside a space that has been around since 1927.

The best time to visit? June, during the Legacy Fest Block Party. It's a celebration with music, food trucks, vendors, and family-friendly fun. Throughout the year, you'll find art shows, historical tours, and events at the rooftop venue.

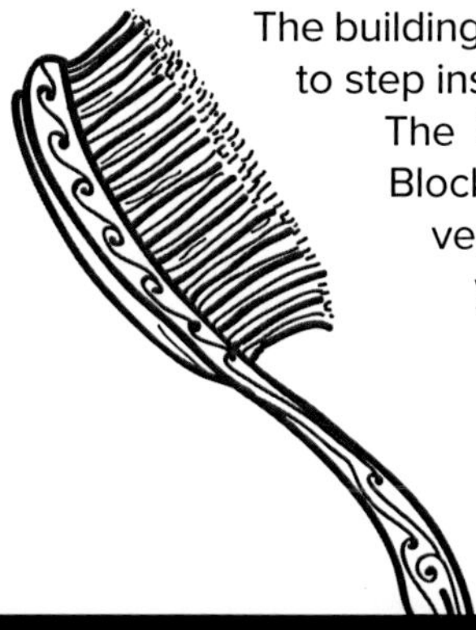

Best Place to Experience Classical Performances

INTERACTIVE MUSIC EVENTS

northcentralorchestras.com
thecenterpresents.org

Music is even more fun when your kids can try the instruments themselves! Some local organizations offer interactive concerts and events where children can do just that, including the beloved Instrument Petting Zoo, where they'll get hands-on with violins, drums, horns, and more.

North Central High School Orchestra hosts its annual Tootsie Pops Concert in January, featuring a pre-show experience where kids can explore instruments before settling in for the music. Your kids will love interacting with the high school musicians.

At the Center for the Performing Arts, the Peanut Butter & Jam Series offers monthly musical mornings for preschoolers, complete with sing-alongs, movement, and plenty of giggles. Sometimes, artists allow attendees to inspect, touch, or try their instruments.

SHAKESPEARE IN THE PARK PERFORMANCES

Various locations in Central Indiana
indyshakes.com
gscindy.org
noblesvillearts.org

Outdoor performances are a magical way to introduce your kids to Shakespeare. Bring your blankets, lawn chairs, and snacks, then kick back and enjoy the show. There's plenty of room for little ones to stretch or wiggle around if they get antsy.

In Central Indiana, several groups make Shakespeare family-friendly and totally free. Indy Shakes presents professional productions at the Taggart Memorial Amphitheatre in Riverside Park. Garfield Shakespeare Company performs two shows a year, including a fall favorite at the MacAllister Amphitheater in Garfield Park. The Noblesville Cultural Arts Commission hosts the longest-running Shakespeare in the Park series at Federal Hill Commons.

INDIANAPOLIS SYMPHONY ORCHESTRA

45 Monument Cir., Indianapolis
(317) 639-4300
indianapolissymphony.org

There are lots of ways for your family to enjoy the Indianapolis Symphony Orchestra, whether you're listening in the audience or playing an instrument yourself. The ISO offers student tickets at a very discounted price, making it easy to introduce your kids to live classical music.

For little ones, the Teddy Bear Concert Series is designed for ages 3-7 but fun for everyone. These free 30-minute shows blend storytelling, movement, and live music to introduce instruments in a kid-friendly way. Afterward, children can meet the musicians and even try a real violin.

The ISO hosts a summer concert series at Conner Prairie called Symphony on the Prairie. Families flock to these performances all season long to enjoy the music, the atmosphere, and the unforgettable outdoor experience.

If you're interested in learning music together, the Metropolitan Youth Orchestra is a special program where kids and their grown-ups take lessons, join an orchestra, and perform. Several of its programs offer placements for older youth with prior experience, and do not require parental participation.

Best Toy Treasure Trove

THE TOY PIT

3827 N College Ave., Indianapolis
(317) 703-8697
yourtoypit.com

The Toy Pit is Indianapolis's largest toy store, and it's packed to the rafters with nostalgia and fun. Outside, you'll spot pop culture murals on the building. Inside, you'll explore 13,000 square feet of toys, action figures, games, and collectibles from classics like Star Wars, Transformers, and Marvel.

Whether you're a lifelong collector or just curious, it's easy to spend hours exploring the display cases and shelves full of hidden treasures. The Toy Pit buys, sells, and trades, so there's always something new. There's even pinball machines and an arcade-style basketball game to keep the kids happily entertained while you take a trip down memory lane.

GOODIES & GIGGLES

811 Massachusetts Ave., Indianapolis
(317) 298-1226
goodiesandgiggles.com

Goodies & Giggles is the kind of place you'll have to drag your kids out of with promises of chocolate or "we'll come back tomorrow." This locally loved toy shop has all the classic toys that last forever and all the trendy favorites splashed across social media. Bonus: there's a real-life bank vault in the back of the store. Be sure to take a peek!

Stumped on what to get for a birthday or holiday? Ask the staff—they're full of brilliant ideas. Plus, they offer free gift wrapping on everything (which is a lifesaver if you've never figured out how to wrap a basketball). Check the website for fun in-store events and activities.

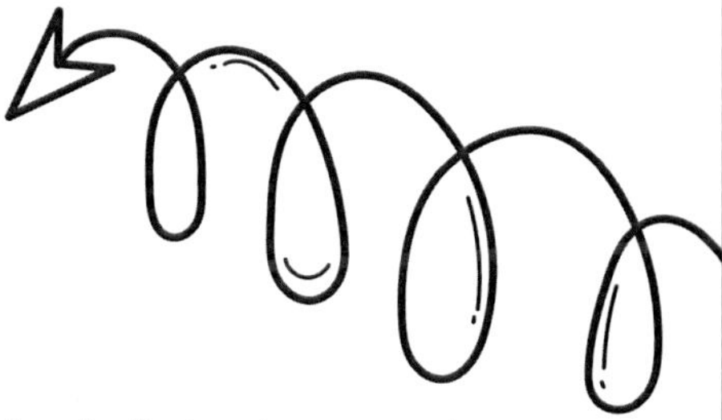

4 KIDS BOOKS & TOYS

4450 Weston Pointe Dr., Zionsville
(317) 733-8710
4kidsbooks.indielite.org

4 Kids Books & Toys is a bright and welcoming indie bookstore and toy shop that's all about sparking imagination. You'll find a fantastic selection of new books and educational toys for kids of all ages, from toddlers to teens. It's the perfect spot to celebrate a milestone or reward your child with something special.

Regular events, like story times and author signings, make this place a favorite for local families. The friendly staff goes above and beyond to help you find the perfect book or toy. New releases for kids and young adults are regularly hitting the shelves, so there's something fresh to discover every visit.

Best Place for Hands-On Activities

ABBY'S GARDEN PARTIES

40 E Poplar St., Zionsville
(317) 670-3623
abbysgardenparties.com

Abby's Garden Parties is a DIY terrarium bar and plant shop where your whole family can create personalized mini gardens together. Start by choosing your favorite succulents, then add soil, a pot, and all the decorative accessories you need to build your terrarium garden. The shop has everything ready for you—just bring your imagination!

The friendly staff will guide you through the planting process, making it fun and age-appropriate for everyone. You'll leave with your very own terrarium and a few handy tips about plant care and the benefits of adding greenery indoors. After you wrap up, take time to explore the adorable shops and cafés in downtown Zionsville.

HOPEANCHOR&CREW

13225 Levinson Ln., Suite 200, Noblesville
(317) 219-6267
hopeanchorandcrew.com

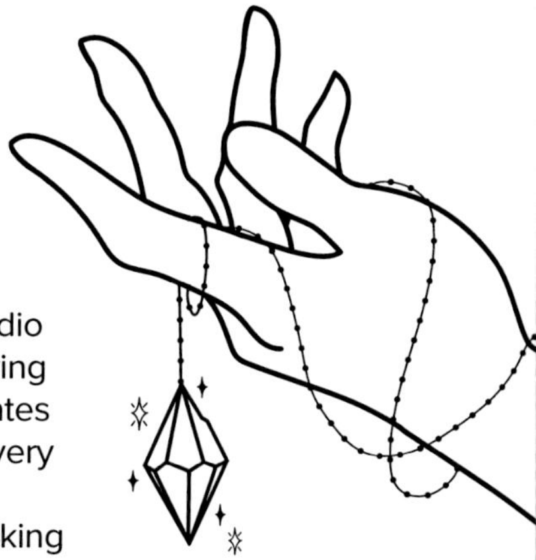

HopeAnchor&Crew is a philanthropic jewelry studio where families can be creative together while giving back to meaningful causes. This nonprofit creates handmade jewelry and donates a portion of every purchase to local and global charities.

Walk right in for a hands-on bracelet-making session, no reservation needed. Each person can design their own creation using a rainbow of beads and charms from the colorful Bead Bar. It's a fun way to take a break from shopping or grab some time together before or after a meal at Hamilton Town Center.

The shop also hosts special events and birthday parties, so be sure to check the schedule for more ways to get crafty and do some good.

IGNITE STUDIO AT HAMILTON EAST PUBLIC LIBRARY

5 Municipal Dr., Fishers
(317) 579-0331
ignite.hamiltoneastpl.org

Makers, builders, crafters, and creators: this is your happy place. Ignite Studio is a free art and maker space filled with tools, machines, and supplies to bring your boldest ideas to life. Some equipment requires a quick training session, and a few tools need a local or statewide library card, but most spaces are ready to dive into.

Want to paint, draw, or sculpt? Grab a maker kit stocked with supplies for cool projects like watercolor painting, clay modeling, and more. The Fab Lab has 3D printers and a laser engraver, and the Audio/Visual Studio has everything you need to record music, broadcast a podcast, make videos, or experiment with a green screen.

Many materials are provided, but for some projects, you might need to bring your own or purchase a few extras from the library.

Best Experiential Art Outing

MUSICAL SWINGS

Fort Ben Cultural Campus, 8950 Otis Ave., Indianapolis

Designed by the internationally acclaimed Montreal-based team Daily Tous Les Jours, this permanent art installation brings music and play together in the most magical way. The Musical Swings at the Fort Ben Cultural Campus in Lawrence aren't your average playground swings; each one plays a musical note as you glide back and forth. When everyone swings together, a beautiful melody fills the air. It's like being part of a giant, interactive instrument. Bonus: The swings light up at night for an extra sprinkle of magic.

The campus also features shaded seating areas, picnic spots, large swinging benches, and several interactive art installations that reflect the history of the area. Fort Harrison State Park is just minutes away, and nearby restaurants make it easy to turn your visit into a full-day adventure.

Bonus: The swings light up at night for an extra sprinkle of magic.

COXHALL CHILDREN'S GARDEN

11677 Towne Rd., Carmel

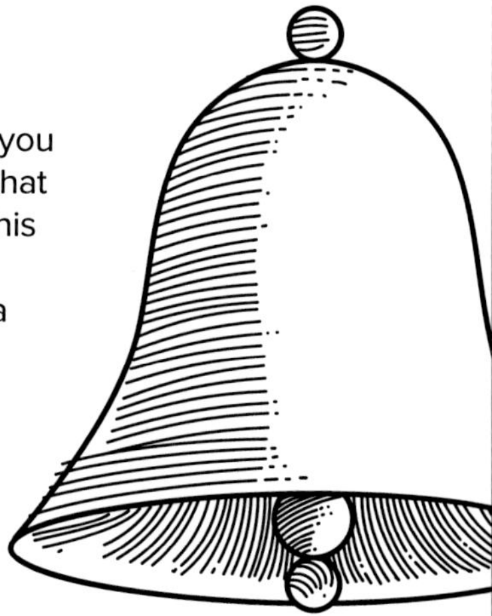

It's easy to miss the gates to Coxhall Gardens, but you can't miss the towering twin 90-foot bell towers that chime every hour, adding even more appeal to this already alluring park.

Wander past walking trails, water features, and a music pavilion to find the whimsical Children's Garden, a dreamy spot where imagination runs free. Instead of slides and monkey bars, you'll discover grassy hills with built-in tunnels, rainbow paths, little bridges, and adorable playhouses that resemble a tiny village.

Beautiful plants and specialty gardens are complemented by playful sculptures and decor. Kids especially love the giant sand area that's perfect for digging and building. Just don't forget to bring your own sand toys!

VIRGINIA B. FAIRBANKS ART & NATURE PARK: 100 ACRES

1850 W 38th St., Indianapolis
discovernewfields.org

If your family loves art, nature, and wide-open spaces, the Virginia B. Fairbanks Art & Nature Park: 100 Acres at Newfields is a must-visit. This 100-acre art and nature park has forests, meadows, a 35-acre lake, and trails perfect for walking or exploring. Admission and parking are free, which makes it even better.

Throughout the park, you'll discover large-scale art installations kids love. One favorite is *Funky Bones*, a giant skeletal sculpture made famous in *The Fault in Our Stars*. At the Hawryluk Sculpture Green, you'll find unique pieces like the *Oracle of Intimation*, which looks like a house sinking into the earth, perfect for climbing.

Best Place for a Fun Dining Experience

THE CAKE BAKE SHOP

Upper Deck, 799 Hanover Place, Carmel
6515 Carrollton Ave., Indianapolis
(317) 257-2253
thecakebakeshop.com

A visit to the Cake Bake Shop is like stepping into a fairy tale. From the moment your kids walk through the door, they'll be mesmerized by sparkling chandeliers, whimsical decor, and beautiful china. It feels like a celebration, especially during spring and the holidays, when the decor is turned all the way up.

There are sparkles in the air (and sometimes in the food), plus delightful coloring pages and pencils to keep little hands busy. Kids love choosing from beautifully presented cakes and pastries, each one sweeter than the last. The shop also has a walk-up bakery and gift shop where you can grab macarons, cookies, and treats to go.

KURA REVOLVING SUSHI BAR

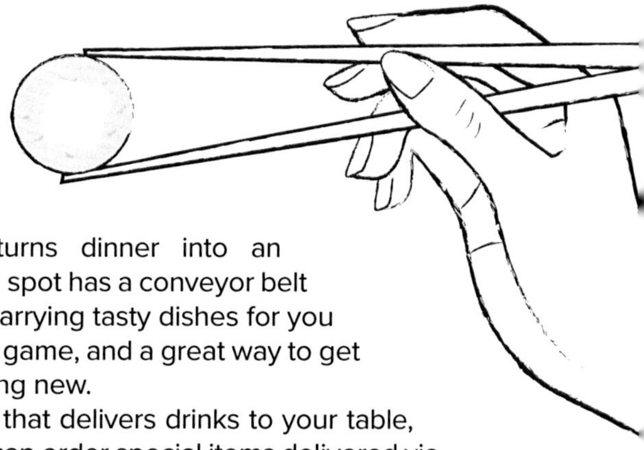

11594 Whistle Dr., Fishers
(463) 270-5570
kurasushi.com

Kura Revolving Sushi Bar turns dinner into an adventure. This high-tech sushi spot has a conveyor belt that winds around the tables, carrying tasty dishes for you to grab as they roll by. It's like a game, and a great way to get kids (and adults) to try something new.

There's also a friendly robot that delivers drinks to your table, and a touchscreen where you can order special items delivered via an express lane conveyor belt. The best part for the kids? For every 15 plates you return after eating, the Bikkura Pon prize machine dispenses a surprise capsule toy that makes dining even more rewarding.

BABY'S

2147 N Talbott St., Indianapolis
(317) 600-3559
babysindy.com

Baby's is a 1950s-style diner with modern flair and a fun, family-friendly atmosphere. Think pink vinyl chairs, glittery countertops, neon lights, and the kind of food everyone loves: smash burgers, broasted chicken, mac & cheese, and milkshakes you'll dream about later.

Kids love playing with the magnetic tiles on the indoor tables, and the outdoor play area is perfect for burning off energy while grown-ups relax on the shaded, pet-friendly patio. There's nothing like a nice summer evening with the sounds of children laughing as you enjoy a beverage. Whether you dine inside or out, it's a great place for a laid-back meal with a retro twist.

Best Snack Stop

LA MICHOACANA PALETERIA

8333 N Michigan Rd., Indianapolis
(317) 405-9264

Authentic Mexican treats are on the menu at La Michoacana, and the bold, colorful flavors are exciting for both kids and adults. The cheerful aesthetic of the shop, complete with big, bright photos of the menu, makes it easy to choose, even if it's your first visit.

La Michoacana offers a huge variety of ice cream and paletas (creamy or fruit-based popsicles). You'll find everything from strawberry and coconut to adventurous picks like mango with chili, tamarind, and even avocado. It's a fantastic place to experience new flavors.

TikTok helped skyrocket the popularity of creations like Dorilocos—Flamin' Hot Doritos topped with melted cheese, jalapeños, peanuts, tomatoes, onions, spices, and more. Maybe your family will inspire the next viral foodie sensation.

LONG'S BAKERY

1453 N Tremont St., Indianapolis
(317) 632-3741
2301 E Southport Rd., Indianapolis
(317) 783-1442
longsbakery.com

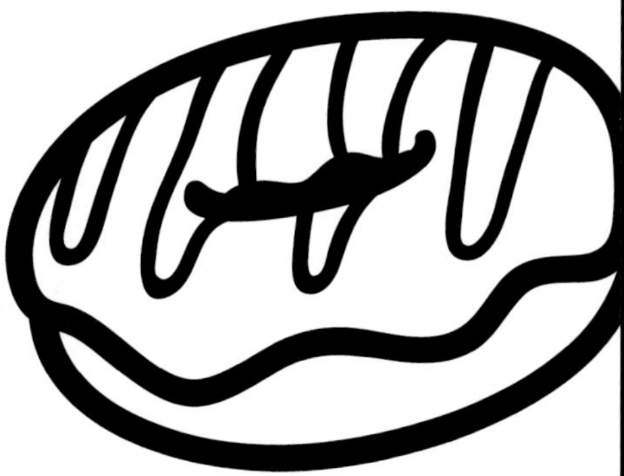

The fragrance of made-from-scratch donuts and sugary glaze greets you at the door of Long's Bakery. This family-owned shop, established in 1955, is a true Indianapolis icon. Most mornings, there's a line out the door with people waiting for their favorites, and in the evening, another group of fans arrives for fresh, warm sweets.

Kids love choosing their own treat or picking a surprise for a friend. While donuts made Long's famous, they also serve up pastries, sweet rolls, pies, cookies, and brownies. Every sweet tooth will be satisfied at Long's. Just don't forget to bring cash; it's the only form of payment accepted!

THE CHEESECAKE LADY INDY

3002 N Illinois St., Indianapolis
(317) 608-7411
thecheesecakeladyindy.com

The Cheesecake Lady Indy has quickly become a local favorite, especially among foodie kids. You can find her six-ounce cheesecake cups at several retail partners during the week, but on weekends, the shop opens and sells fresh cups in flavors like Biscoff, chocolate peanut butter, peach cobbler, and strawberry crunch.

There's something to satisfy every sweet tooth, and it's even more fun when everyone picks a different flavor and shares. If six ounces isn't enough, you can preorder a PAN-Cake or go all out with a 4way Cheesecake.

Once you've picked your favorite, head across the street to play for free at the Seven Wonders of the World garden at The Children's Museum of Indianapolis for some sweet post-dessert playtime.

Best Cool Place for Frozen Treats

MOO & LOU FROZEN TREATS

5645 N Post Rd., Ste. B, Indianapolis
(317) 597-0075
mooloufrozentreats.com

Moo & Lou started as an ice cream truck and has grown into a quirky little shop full of heart. The interior is colorful and inviting with twinkle lights, interactive art, a craft station, and comfy seating that invites families to stay and play.

This family-owned dessert shop supports Maddie Smiles, a nonprofit dedicated to spreading kindness in memory of the owners' daughter, Maddie. It's more than a sweet stop; it's a feel-good experience.

Try the homemade ice cream, dreamsicles, purple cows (grape soda floats), root beer floats with Triple XXX Root Beer, gourmet hot cocoa, baked goods, milkshakes, and more.

BRICS (BROAD RIPPLE ICE CREAM STATION)

901 E 64th St., Indianapolis
(317) 257-5757
bricsindy.com

BRICS, short for Broad Ripple Ice Cream Station, is located inside the historic Monon Railway Station, and it's a local favorite for a reason. During warmer months, you'll love the patio seating, and in winter, the cozy indoor space (complete with a fireplace) is just as inviting.

Right along the Monon Trail, BRICS is the perfect pit stop during a family walk or bike ride. Fill up your water bottles at the refill station, then choose from more than 36 traditional ice cream flavors plus eight vegan or dairy-free options.

Bonus: If your pup tags along, they'll get a free treat.

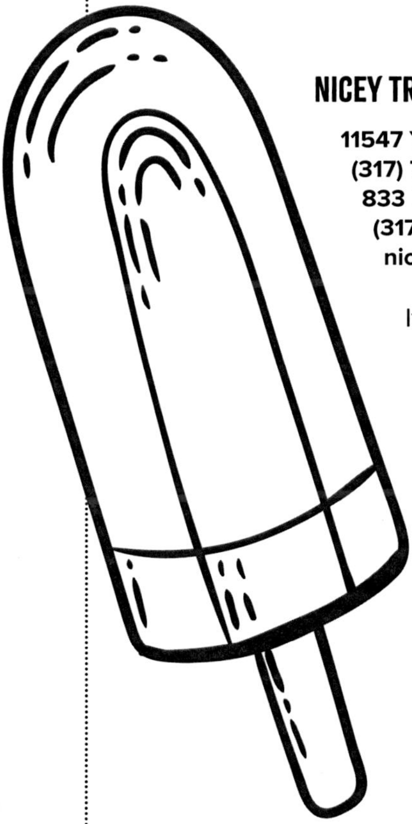

NICEY TREAT

11547 Yard St., Fishers
(317) 712-3908
833 E Westfield Blvd., Indianapolis
(317) 602-6423
niceytreat.com

It's instantly summer when you're holding a popsicle, unless it's a Not So Hot Chocolate pop from Nicey Treat. These handmade, all-natural frozen treats are a favorite at local events and festivals, but you'll find the full lineup of fun flavors at one of the two brick-and-mortar shops.

The unique flavor combinations, like roasted pineapple and basil or blackberry ginger lemonade, make Nicey Treat a great spot for those with elevated taste buds, and the classic flavors like fudge, orange cream, and pink lemonade are favorites for kids (and adults) who just love what they love. Before you go, check store hours—they may be closed depending on the time of year.

Best Way to Stir Up Culinary Creativity

SPROUTS COOKING SCHOOL

11145 N Michigan Rd., Zionsville
13190 Hazel Dell Pkwy., Carmel
(317) 688-7499
sproutscookingschool.com

If you have a kiddo who loves cooking, or you're hoping to spark a culinary passion, Sprouts Cooking School is a must-do. This cooking school is just for kids, complete with kid-sized counters and equipment that will make you swoon. Thematic classes keep things fresh and exciting, while kids learn skills and recipes they can try again at home.

Sign up for single-session classes, MemberChef semester programs, family classes, and seasonal camps. Classes are offered for three age groups: Tiny (ages 3-5), Junior (ages 6-8), and Tween (ages 9-13). Sprouts Cooking School also has birthday party packages with themes like Perfectly Paris, Enchanted Unicorns, and Cupcake Battles.

SUR LA TABLE FAMILY FUN COOKING

14400 Clay Terrace Blvd., Carmel
(317) 575-0953
surlatable.com

Plan ahead and hop online to sign up for a Family Fun Cooking Class at Sur La Table's retail store. Kids ages 7 and up can join themed classes with their grown-ups in attendance. Together, you'll create a variety of dishes, from appetizers to desserts, under the guidance of professional chefs.

You'll learn cooking techniques while building confidence in the kitchen. The recipes are easy to re-create at home, so the fun doesn't have to stop when class ends.

During the summer, there's a Kids & Teens Cooking Series, a week-long session with classes that meet for two hours each day. Young chefs learn new cooking techniques and get hands-on experience with cuisines from around the world.

MAGGIANO'S LITTLE ITALY KIDS COOKING CLASSES

3550 E 86th St., Indianapolis
(317) 814-0700
maggianos.com

The best part about Maggiano's Kids Cooking Classes might just be the lunch buffet! It's designed for ages 5-11, but children outside of that age range are invited to join as well. The class includes a cooking lesson and a delicious meal. Each child must be accompanied by a ticketed adult.

Kids meet at the restaurant in the morning and learn how to prepare Italian favorites like Maggiano's famous lasagna, meatloaf cupcakes, and mini apple pies. After class, families enjoy the lunch buffet together. Child tickets include the class and buffet; adult tickets include the buffet only.

Classes are held periodically throughout the year and are popular, so keep an eye on the event calendar.

Best Brewery or Winery with a Kid-Friendly Space

DANIEL'S FAMILY VINEYARD & WINERY

9061 N 700 W, McCordsville
(317) 248-5222
danielsvineyard.com

Indiana is home to many wineries, and many are family friendly, but Daniel's welcomes families on another level. Its calendar is packed with events, from live music and trivia nights to holiday parties and grape-stomping fun.

Families can enjoy outdoor games, dancing on the lawn, and children's concerts on select days. Kids are often seen climbing the hill, rolling down it, and giggling their way through the vineyard's open green space while adults sip and relax. There are tables with bonfires built into them and even a picnic table area.

The food menu is kid-friendly, with pizzas, breadsticks, juice boxes, and even non-alcoholic slushies.

MASHCRAFT BREWERY

11069 Allisonville Rd., Fishers
(317) 863-5165

2205 N Delaware St., Indianapolis
(317) 602-2552

1140 N State Rd. 135, Greenwood
(317) 215-4578
mashcraft.com

MashCraft has such a welcoming atmosphere for families. Spacious seating areas, high chairs, and booster seats make it easy to bring the whole crew. They've even stocked up on board games and card games to keep kids entertained.

The menu includes crowd-pleasers like soft pretzels, chicken tenders, and personal pizzas, perfect for picky eaters. Adults can sip craft beer while kids enjoy soft drinks, lemonade, or juice. On warm days, the patio is a great place to sit, and some locations host kid-themed events like KidCrafts or Santa visits in December. It's a great restaurant where both kids and parents can relax and have a good time together.

URBAN VINES WINERY AND BREWERY

303 E 161st St., Westfield
(317) 763-0678
urban-vines.com

Just a hop away from Grand Park, families enjoy spending time at Urban Vines. Adults can enjoy handcrafted wines, beers, and slushies, while kids love the big lawn, pond, and wooden playground.

Live music and events add to the fun, and charcuterie boards and snack trays make it easy to grab a bite. Rent a bonfire ring to stay warm or create a cozy space to hang out with family and friends. Bring a picnic blanket or lawn chairs and settle in with your favorite drink while the kids play games or toss a ball around.

Best Place for a Kid-Friendly Caffeine Break

HITHERTO COFFEE & GAMING PARLOUR

1558 N State St., Greenfield
(317) 318-9782
hithertocoffee.com

Friendly coffee shop meets board game wonderland: that's Hitherto in a nutshell. With hundreds of games in the lending library, you'll always find something fun to play, whether it's an old favorite or a new one to learn together. Plus, your kids will be participating in a screen-free activity.

The kid-friendly menu includes cotton candy frappes, orange dreamsicle smoothies, pastries, and light bites. The café atmosphere is laid-back and playful, making it easy to hang out as a family. Often, there are game releases and learn-to-play events; check the website for details.

Seating is first-come, first-served, but if you want to guarantee a table during peak times, you can reserve one for a small fee, which goes toward food and drinks.

Plus, your kids will be participating in a screen-free activity.

THE BUSY BEE PLAY CAFE

5635 W 96th St., Suite 200, Indianapolis
(317) 456-7898
thebusybeeplaycafe.com

For adults, Busy Bee is a coffee shop, but kids know it's one of the best indoor play spaces Indianapolis has to offer. It's meant for toddlers through age 8, with a daily play fee that lets you come and go throughout the day.

There's a multi-level play structure with slides and tunnels; an open floor space for building and moving; and a mini city with a diner, post office, and fire station. Babies and younger toddlers can explore their own soft play area, train table, and cozy reading spots.

Reservations are recommended, especially when it's nicer indoors than outdoors.

URBAN BREW

78 E Morgan St., Martinsville
(765) 341-4305
urbanbrewcoffee.com

Urban Brew Coffee is the perfect blend for parents and kids. Grab a coffee and a croffle (that's a croissant-waffle hybrid) for yourself, and treat the kids to playtime. This cozy little café isn't just about amazing lattes (but definitely try the baklava latte); it also has an indoor play area just for kids.

The play zone is designed for babies, toddlers, and preschoolers. It's a shoe-free space with a 10-kid max, so it never feels crowded. Parents stay nearby and keep watch; think of it as a hands-on play café experience.

There's even a kids' drink menu with fun options like the Under the Sea Sipper and the Birthday Cake Blender.

Best Way to Satisfy a Sweet Tooth

DEBRAND FINE CHOCOLATES

8685 River Crossing Blvd., Indianapolis
(317) 669-0955
debrand.com

There's nothing quite like walking into a chocolate shop. The fragrance of cacao, butter, sugar, and milk delights the senses and tickles your nose. It's the kind of sensory overload that kids can really get behind.

Choose from a delightful array of chocolates in the glass display case, from classic milk chocolates to unique truffles, or order from the specialty menu. The famous DeBrand customizable chocolate sundae is a family favorite. Adults can caffeinate with a hot or iced drink or go all in with an affogato, which is basically an espresso sundae.

Tall tables are near the front, and more relaxed booths and lower table seating are tucked in the back of the store.

ZAHARAKOS ICE CREAM PARLOR AND MUSEUM

329 Washington St., Columbus
(812) 378-1900
zaharakos.com

Zaharakos has been serving guests since 1900 and offers a true early 20th-century soda fountain experience. The menu has burgers, house-made ice creams, sundaes, and sodas that are crafted by soda jerks using syrup and carbonated water from the original 1904 onyx soda fountain.

Adjacent to the dining room is a museum filled with pre-1900 soda fountains, syrup dispensers, and mechanical music players. Bring quarters! You'll want to hear the self-playing organs and the kids' favorite: the Banjo Orchestra. Everyone will be fascinated as metal brackets pluck banjo strings, accompanied by a piano, snare drum, tambourine, triangle, wood block, castanets, bass drum, and cymbal.

LIBBY'S ICE CREAM & GIFTS

222 W Broadway St., Fortville
(317) 496-4576
220 W Mill St., Greenfield
(317) 477-4092
libbysfrozentreats.com

If sweet treats are the name of the game, Libby's Ice Cream is winning. Both locations serve a rotating selection of hand-dipped, locally sourced ice cream from Sundae's Homemade Ice Cream in Indianapolis. Ice cream cones, sundaes, banana splits, milkshakes, malts, smoothies, and root beer floats are among your choices. Try Libby's Pink Elephant ice cream, named for Fortville's beloved mascot.

In Fortville, there's plenty of indoor seating, a gift shop, and a party room. The Greenfield location is within the Depot Street Park right off the Pennsy Trail. There's a convenient walk-up window, plus indoor and patio seating. Dairy-free options are available at both locations.

Best Place to Visit Nature Indoors

HOLLIDAY PARK NATURE CENTER

6363 Spring Mill Rd., Indianapolis
(317) 327-7180
hollidaypark.org

If your family is looking for free, hands-on nature experiences, Holliday Park Nature Center is a must-visit. It's full of kid-friendly activities designed to make learning about nature fun. Kids can crawl through a giant tree; observe bees, turtles, and snakes; and explore nature-themed play areas. Stop in at the bird and wildlife observation area to watch the feeders and listen in through the sound system.

The 94-acre park has scenic hiking trails, local wildlife, and an architectural feature called the Ruins. A nearby playground and splash pad make it easy to turn your visit into a full day of outdoor fun.

GARFIELD PARK CONSERVATORY

2505 Conservatory Dr., Indianapolis
(317) 327-7183
garfieldgardensconservatory.org

Nature, learning, and a sprinkle of magic come together at the Garfield Park Conservatory. Located within Indy's oldest city park, this hidden gem is a tropical sanctuary. Admission is just a few dollars per person, making it the most budget-friendly tropical vacation around.

You'll be wowed by towering palms, dazzling flowers, and exotic plants from across the globe. It's warm year-round, so it's an especially great escape during colder months.

Kids love spotting bananas on the trees, finding koi in the pond, visiting reptiles, and walking behind the indoor waterfall. Scavenger hunts and seasonal displays add even more adventure.

COOL CREEK PARK NATURE CENTER

2000 E 151st St., Carmel
(317) 774-2500
hamiltoncounty.in.gov

Cool Creek Park Nature Center is a family-friendly educational hub within the beautiful 90-acre park. It's a great spot to visit before or after exploring the park's four miles of wooded trails.

Inside, kids can learn all about Indiana's woodlands and the importance of preserving natural habitats. Exhibits and live animal displays, including turtles and snakes, are always a hit. Young nature lovers look forward to programs like story times, animal encounters, and guided hikes.

Outside, the Nature Play Area invites kids to climb, build, and explore in a natural setting for a time of creativity and unstructured play.

Best Indoor Fun for Little Ones

DIG DIG FOR KIDS

12800 Ford Dr., Fishers
(317) 827-2087
digdigforkids.com

If your kids can't get enough of diggers, dump trucks, and sand, Dig Dig for Kids is their dream come true. This 1,100-square-foot indoor sandbox is filled with soft, clean sand and all the shovels, buckets, and toy excavators they'll need to dig and build for hours. Since this space is indoors, rain or shine, it's a lot of fun and never a muddy mess.

Parents can relax in the cozy seating area with free Wi-Fi while the kids play. No need to bring toys; everything is provided. It is designed for children 10 and under, but older siblings are welcome too, as long as they're respectful of younger kids.

KID CITY AT GREENWOOD COMMUNITY CENTER

100 Surina Way, Greenwood
(317) 881-4545
greenwood.in.gov

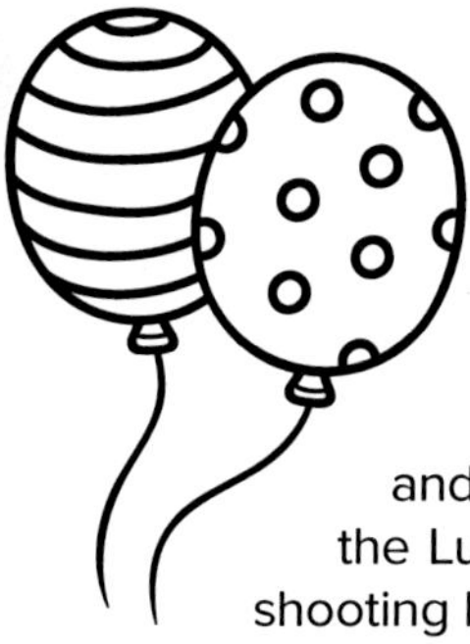

Kid City is the perfect place for kids to burn off energy, especially when the weather isn't cooperating or it's just time for an inside day. Located inside the Greenwood Community Center, this two-story indoor play space is great for both active and imaginative play.

Downstairs, you'll find a toddler playground, climbing structures, and building supplies. Upstairs are interactive walls and floors, a pretend grocery store and kitchen, an art studio, and the Luckey Climber that spans both levels. There's even a gym for shooting hoops.

Kid City is ideal for children 12 and under. Grown-ups will love the comfy seating, free Wi-Fi, and super-affordable admission (it's free with a Greenwood Community Center membership).

KID'S PLANET

499 Southpoint Cir., Brownsburg
(317) 350-2095
kidsplanetfun.com

Kid's Planet features a massive four-story play structure with slides, tunnels, ball shooters, and plenty of space to play and explore. There are endless opportunities for hiding and playing tag with siblings or making new friends.

There's a dedicated toddler area for children 4 and under, with padded play equipment and a small plush carousel. This area is safely sectioned off and gives younger kids their own space to play comfortably.

Outside the play space, you'll find an arcade with video games, claw machines, and skill games that offer prize tickets. There's also a concession area, which offers a variety of food and drinks, and free Wi-Fi is available.

Best Place for Big Kids to Play Indoors

SLICK CITY ACTION PARK

4430 N County Rd.
1000 E, Brownsburg
(317) 936-3436
slickcity.com

Slick City Action Park is an indoor playground with massive slides. The park uses a special dry-slide technology, replicating the thrills of a water slide without water. It's year-round fun in a climate-controlled environment.

The 42,000-square-foot facility has a variety of slides. Among them is Fast Lane, a side-by-side slide so families can race; the Royal Flush, which spins riders through a swirling bowl before dropping them through the center; and Mega Launch, which propels participants into the air before landing on a soft mat.

Play a game of basketball with extra hops on a floor pad filled with air, plus a trapeze, swing, and zipline. Younger guests under 45 inches tall will love the Junior Jungle, a separate play zone with climbing structures and pint-sized slides.

SKY ZONE TRAMPOLINE PARK

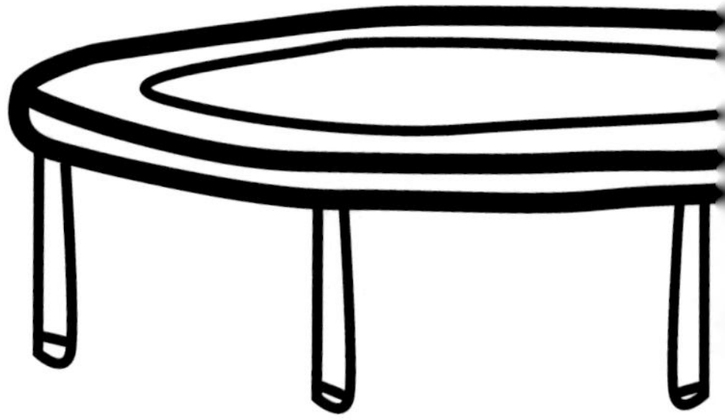

4150 Kildeer Dr., Indianapolis
(317) 759-9925

8356 Masters Rd. N, Indianapolis
(317) 520-5030

851 S Columbia Rd., Ste 172, Plainfield
(317) 268-3200
skyzone.com

Known for their wall-to-wall trampolines, Sky Zone is a go-to for families who love to bounce. The entire facility is packed with trampoline fun, including dodgeball courts, ninja warrior courses, foam pits, and basketball trampolines.

For younger kids, Toddler Time offers a quieter session without big kids around. Sky Zone also hosts glow-in-the-dark jump nights and sensory-friendly hours and offers memberships and birthday party packages.

Be sure to check what attractions your location offers, and don't forget—everyone needs Sky Socks to jump.

URBAN AIR ADVENTURE PARK

1172 N Main St., Franklin
(317) 207-0920

14450 Mundy Dr., Noblesville
(317) 565-2035

392 Plainfield Commons Dr., Plainfield
(463) 888-9106
urbanair.com

Urban Air is the place to go for kids who have energy to burn. From wall-to-wall trampolines to climbing walls and obstacle courses, there's something for every thrill-seeker. Kids can bounce, flip, and test their ninja skills on the warrior course; bounce in the dodgeball arena; or take flight on the Sky Rider zip line.

Younger kids love the multi-level indoor playground, while older kids gravitate toward the battle beams and slam dunk courts.

Admission prices vary depending on which attractions you choose, so check before you go. Parents can join the action, or chill in the lounge with free Wi-Fi. Preschool times and sensory-friendly hours are scheduled each month.

Best Location for a Birthday Bash

SMILEY INDOOR PLAYGROUND & ARCADE

5729 E 86th St., Indianapolis
(317) 286-2625
smileyindianapolis.com

At 25,000 square feet, Smiley is an enormous indoor playland with something for everyone, from toddlers to big kids. The main attraction is the giant ball pit that calls to kids the moment they walk in. Giant slides, a separate toddler play area, and sensory spaces are all part of the fun.

There are also interactive wall and floor games, virtual reality, and a full arcade. Parents can relax in the café while the kids explore every inch of the playground.

Smiley offers party packages with themed private rooms, and admission is based on playtime duration, from one hour to all day. Smiley grip socks are required.

GAME SHOW BATTLE ROOMS

5753 E 86th St., Indianapolis
(317) 348-1344
gameshowbattlerooms.com

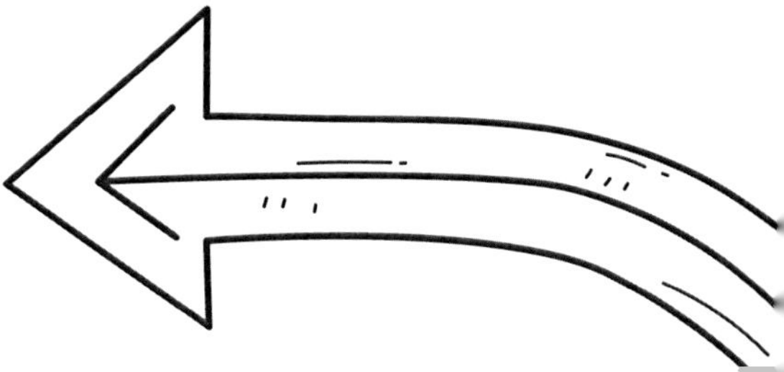

If you've ever dreamed of putting your family in the spotlight on a real game show, this activity is for you. Face off against friends or relatives in a state-of-the-art studio-style arena equipped with buzzers, lights, and props that feel straight out of a game show set.

Teams are guided by a live host through fast-paced challenges and trivia rounds. The games are hilarious, competitive, and full of surprises.

It's perfect for birthdays, group outings, or just a memorable family night. Group sizes range from 8 to over 60 people, and because there are a variety of games, most kids of school age will enjoy the battle.

MALIBU JACK'S INDOOR THEME PARK

2415 Sagamore Pkwy. S, Lafayette
(765) 799-0001
malibujacks.net

Malibu Jack's in Lafayette is an impressive indoor amusement park and entertainment center. Whether your crew is into racing, laser tag, arcade games, or mini golf, you'll find it here, and there's a special play area just for kids 10 and under.

The top attractions include an indoor go-kart track, a multi-level laser tag arena, mini golf, and bowling. They even have the Twist-N-Shout Coaster, an indoor spinning roller coaster with a bit of a thrill. The arcade is full of fun, skill-based games for all ages, with prizes. Birthday parties at Malibu Jack's are a great time for everyone.

Best Free Indoor Playground

THE TREEHOUSE INDOOR PLAYGROUND

800 Dan Jones Rd., Plainfield
(317) 839-2384
plainfieldchristian.com

Located inside Plainfield Christian Church, the Treehouse Indoor Playground is a fun and attractive space with a treehouse-themed play structure. There are slides, climbers, and plenty of nooks and crannies to explore. It's open to kids ages 2 to 12 during designated play hours each week.

Kids love the ride-on toys, building sets, and hidden play treasures scattered throughout. The space is encapsulated by large floor to ceiling windows, allowing natural lighting to brighten the space. Parents appreciate the complimentary coffee and comfy seating throughout the play area.

THE CENTER AT NORTHVIEW CHRISTIAN CHURCH

623 N State Rd. 39, Danville
(317) 745-5990
northviewchristian.org

Open to the public seven days a week, the Center at Northview Christian Church is great for indoor playtime. Bring your whole family or meet up with your favorite friends. The multi-level playground includes swings, slides, climbing areas, and bouncy seats. There's even an indoor turf field for open play and yard games.

Parents often take advantage of the indoor walking track to sneak in some steps, or grab a coffee from Fields Coffee, the on-site café. Free Wi-Fi is available throughout the building. Socks are required for all play areas.

THE PARK AT TRADERS POINT CHRISTIAN CHURCH

6590 S Indianapolis Rd., Whitestown
(317) 769-5557
tpcc.org

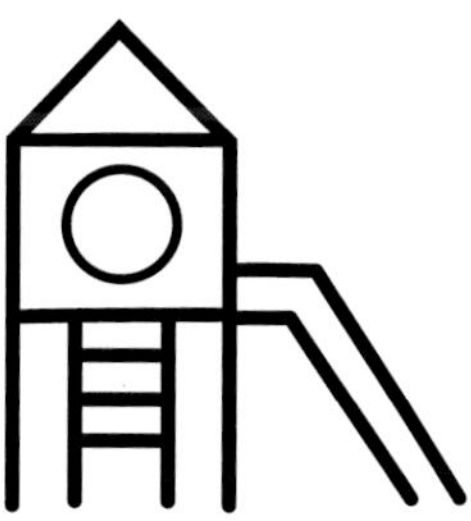

The Park at Traders Point Christian Church is home to a spacious indoor playground with a five-story playscape packed with slides, climbing walls, and even a mini zip line. A separate toddler zone, designed for kids 3 and under, includes small equipment and soft surfaces for safe exploration.

Parents can relax at nearby picnic tables, perfect for snacks, supervision, or even sneaking in a little laptop time. The space is bright, welcoming, and open to the public for free. Just remember: shoes off, socks on. Call your friends and meet up for a playdate at the Park. Check the website for hours, as they vary throughout the week.

Best Way to Try a New Sport

Q SKATE SHOP & INDOOR PARK

1727 Stout Field E Dr., Indianapolis
(317) 498-5299
qskatepark.com

Indianapolis's only indoor skate park has ramps, rails, and ledges built for all skill levels—from first-timers to seasoned boarders. Whether you're a beginner or a seasoned rider, you're invited. It's not just for skateboards; scooters, inline skates, and quad skates are welcome too.

Helmets are required for anyone under 18, and skateboard and helmet rentals are available in-house. The fully stocked skate shop has helpful staff and everything you need to get started. Group lessons are offered multiple times a week for a small fee, and they host camps every spring, summer, and winter.

ATOMIC DUCKPIN BOWLING

1105 Prospect St., Indianapolis
(317) 686-6010
fountainsquareindy.com

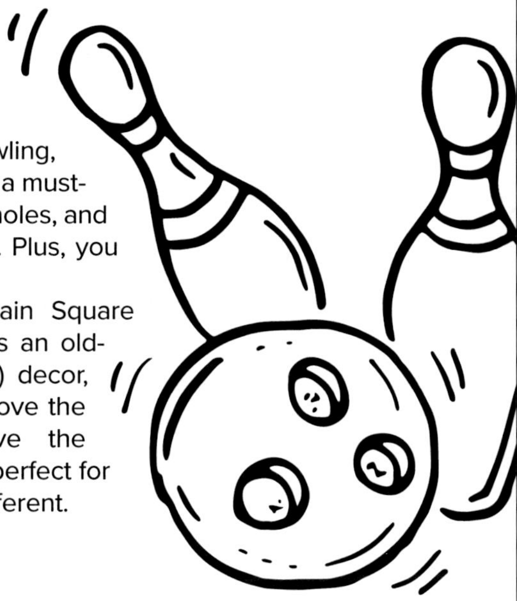

If your family is up for a fun twist on bowling, duckpin bowling in Fountain Square is a must-try. It uses smaller balls without finger holes, and shorter pins, making it easier for kids. Plus, you get three rolls per turn instead of two.

Located inside the historic Fountain Square Theatre building, Atomic Duckpin has an old-school charm with retro (err, original) decor, low lighting, and vintage lanes. Kids love the quirky setup, and grown-ups love the throwback fun. It's an Indy institution, perfect for families who love something a little different.

WINTER CLUB ICE SKATING LESSONS

Pop Weaver Youth Pavilion at the Indiana State Fairgrounds
1202 E 38th St., Indianapolis
winterclubindy.org

The Winter Club of Indianapolis teaches Learn to Skate classes for ages 3 and up, and every ability level is welcome. That means adults and kids can hit the ice, whether you're just starting out or polishing your cool moves. It's a welcoming, supportive environment where skaters learn new skills and build confidence week after week.

Each class typically includes 30 minutes of group instruction and 30 minutes of supervised practice time to try new skills. Skate rental is included. At the end of the season, skaters have the opportunity to perform in a class recital, showcasing all they've learned.

Best Spot for Offbeat Athletics

WILBUR SHAW MEMORIAL SOAP BOX DERBY HILL

2200 W 30th St., Indianapolis
indianapolis.soapboxderby.org

Wilbur Shaw Derby Hill is home to the longest Soap Box Derby track in the country, and it's right here in Indianapolis! Named for the three-time Indy 500 winner, this site hosts youth racers ages 8 to 20 in three divisions: Stock, Super Stock, and Masters. Races occur March through September on select weekends.

Watching the races is a great activity for families who love cars. The top of the hill is a good place to view the action, but any spot along the track gives a front-row seat. Speaking of seats, bring your own. The cars are silent, so even the youngest kids can enjoy the experience without sensory overload. Watching kids race their handcrafted cars is both inspiring and fun.

INDY IGNITE VOLLEYBALL

Fishers Event Center, 11000 Stockdale St., Fishers
provolleyball.com/teams/indy-ignite

Indiana's first professional women's volleyball team has 14 home matches per season at the Fishers Event Center. The women's volleyball season runs from January through May and provides an entertaining, high-energy indoor outing for families during the winter and spring chill. The games are fast-paced, easy to follow, and exciting for all ages. The team is active in the community and committed to growing youth volleyball in Indiana.

The Fishers Event Center also features a KultureCity-certified sensory room with calming amenities like air walls, tactile panels, and other sensory accommodations. Plus, sensory kits are available for guests to use.

HICKORY HALL POLO CLUB

7551 E 100 N, Whitestown
(317) 223-4281
indypolo.com

Kids who love horses and kids who love sports will thoroughly enjoy Hickory Hall Polo Club matches. Polo brings horses, sports, and tailgating together for one of the most unique family outings in Indiana. From June through October, families gather for exciting polo matches during "Polo at Sunset," which benefits local charities.

Kids love the open space to run, the fast-paced action, and the chance to stomp divots between matches. Some nights even include a candy drop from an airplane! Admission is by the carload, so pack the picnic blankets, snacks, and lawn chairs, or grab dinner from food vendors on-site.

Best Place to Tee Off with the Whole Family

BIRDIES MINIATURE GOLF COURSE & SPORTS BAR

632 E State Rd. 32, Westfield
(317) 706-4906
birdiesindy.com

Birdies is a local favorite year-round thanks to its restaurant, with a side of miniature golf. Play 18 or 36 holes on creatively designed courses with water features, rock structures, and lots of entertaining obstacles. While kids of all ages will have fun, it's best suited for ages 5 and up; 18 of the holes are wheelchair accessible.

During the holidays, Birdies dresses up the course for Christmas with lights and decorations for winter mini-golf under the stars. After playing, head indoors to warm up with yummy food and drinks from the restaurant.

BACK 9

1415 Drover St., Indianapolis
(317) 912-0920
back9golf.com

This multi-level golf venue is a high-tech driving range with target games and ball-tracking technology. Think driving range meets arcade meets bowling, all in climate-controlled bays, perfect for year-round play.

Kids love interactive games like Bullseye, where they aim at giant targets to score points, and Longest Drive to see who can hit the farthest. Don't worry about keeping score; Back 9's system does all the measuring and tabulating for you. Even if your kids have never touched a golf club (they have child-size clubs available), the simple scoring system and giant targets make it easy and exciting. Advance reservations are recommended.

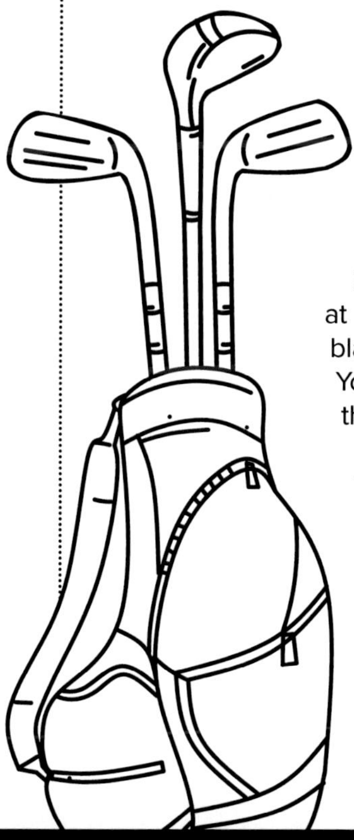

TOPGOLF

9200 E 116th St., Fishers
(765) 212-3488
topgolf.com

Forget stuffy country clubs—tee up for high-tech fun at Topgolf Fishers. This interactive driving range is a blast for both beginners and experienced golfers. You'll hit microchipped golf balls at giant targets on the field, and every shot is tracked for instant scoring. Kids love watching their points add up on screen in the bay as they compete in games. With climate-controlled bays and comfy seating, the whole family can play or be a spectator and cheer everyone on. Topgolf has clubs for kids and adults, or you can bring your own. With so many game modes and targets, even first-timers will feel confident.

Best Spot for Fishing Fun

FREEDOM PARK

850 W Stop 18 Rd., Greenwood
greenwood.in.gov

Just beyond the bridge and along the walking trail on the south end of Freedom Park, you'll find a quiet, kid-friendly fishing spot. It's a great place to introduce children to the fun of fishing, with a pond stocked with bluegill, largemouth bass, and even a rare albino catfish.

Anglers 18 and older need a valid Indiana fishing license to cast a line here. Greenwood Parks and Recreation often hosts a kids' fishing derby, making it even more exciting for young anglers. When they're ready for a change of pace, the park offers playgrounds and plenty of other ways to play.

FLAT FORK CREEK PARK

16141 E 101st St., Fishers
playfishers.com

Flat Fork Creek Park is a nature-lover's dream, with wooded BMX trails and an elevated boardwalk that leads to treehouses and lookout towers. It's a year-round favorite, perfect for exploring in warm weather and ideal for sledding when it snows (there's even a sled borrowing station!).

Within the park is a catch-and-release fishing pond perfect for family fishing. The pond is stocked with sunfish and largemouth bass, and while anyone 18+ needs a license to fish most days, Indiana offers a few Free Fishing Days each year when licenses aren't required. Some parks, including Flat Fork Creek, host special events with loaner gear and fishing help for beginners.

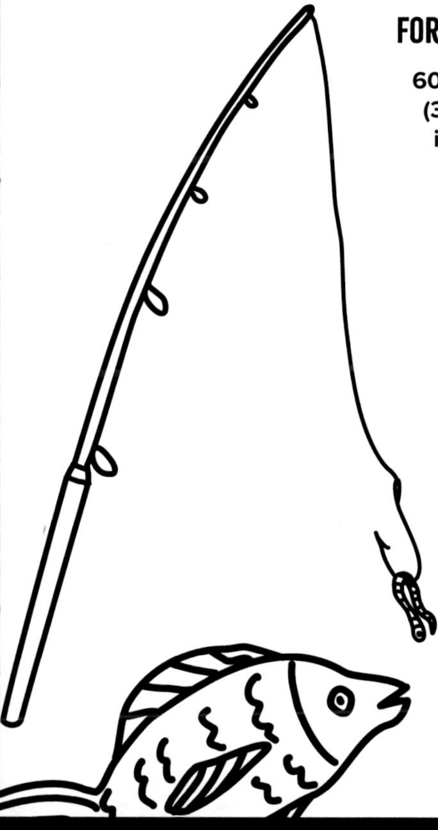

FORT HARRISON STATE PARK

6000 N Post Rd., Indianapolis
(317) 591-0904
in.gov/fortharrison

Just outside downtown Indy, Fort Harrison State Park is a peaceful retreat, and Delaware Lake is its go-to fishing spot. The lake is stocked with bluegill, bass, and catfish, and the calm waters and shoreline make it perfect for beginners. Bring your own gear, and anyone 18+ will need a valid Indiana fishing license.

Want to get the kids comfortable before hitting the lake? Visit the Indiana Department of Natural Resources building during the State Fair. There's a special kids' fishing pond and free fishing programs to help them learn. Plus, they can use their new skills and try to reel in a fish at the fair.

Best Pickleball Playground in Town

GREENWOOD PARKS AND RECREATION

Multiple locations
(317) 881-4545
greenwood.in.gov

No city in Indiana has embraced the pickleball craze quite like Greenwood. The Parks and Recreation Department has set the bar high with both indoor and outdoor courts that are open to the public and tournament-ready.

Freedom Park Pickleball Complex (850 W Stop 18 Rd.) has 16 outdoor courts built for sanctioned tournament play. They're open to the public every day, from dawn to dusk.

The Greenwood Community Center (100 Surina Way) offers four indoor wood-surface courts with permanent lines and portable nets. Open play is available on select days and evenings with a membership, or grab a day pass.

Over at the Greenwood Fieldhouse (411 S Madison Ave.), you'll find four indoor hard courts. Members and day pass guests can access these courts during designated hours.

3RD SHOT PICKLEBALL

4400 W 96th St., Carmel
(317) 377-4024
3rdshotpickleball.com/home-indy

Whether you're a seasoned player or brand new to the court, 3rd Shot Pickleball is a top-notch indoor facility that caters to all skill levels. It's a great place for families to play, learn, and improve together, rain or shine.

3rd Shot Pickleball hosts a variety of events throughout the year, including blacklight pickleball nights, youth tournaments, and open play sessions. Special AI cameras even record your matches and create highlight clips you can share online.

Summer camps, lessons, and youth programs are available to help kids build skills and confidence on the court. Plus, it's a blast for parents, too.

KEPHART PARK

3936 W County Rd. 144, Bargersville
bargersvillein.myrec.com

Kephart Park is a favorite local hangout for pickler families. The eight dedicated, fenced-in courts are first-come, first-served, no reservations or fees required. Just bring your own paddles and family teammates and get ready to dink.

The courts are asphalt surfaces and have painted lines and nets. If you're bringing a cheering squad, there are bleachers along the court perimeter. Just note: they're uncovered, so don't forget sunscreen or shade gear. There's parking near the courts, plus bathrooms and a drinking fountain. Between matches, little ones can enjoy the colorful playground, take a walk on the trails, or splash around in the seasonal splash pad.

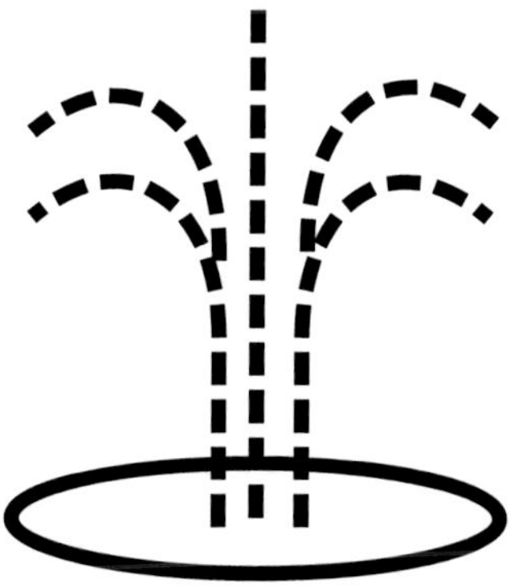

Best Way to Experience Football Up Close

INDIANAPOLIS COLTS TRAINING CAMP

Grand Park Sports Campus,
19000 Grand Park Blvd., Westfield
colts.com

NFL fans, cheerleading enthusiasts, mascot admirers, and everyone in between love attending the Indianapolis Colts Training Camp. This annual summer event enables fans of all ages to watch the team prepare for the upcoming NFL season.

Attendees can sit in the stands to watch practice sessions; participate in interactive activities; meet cheerleaders; get to know Blue, the Colts' mascot; and mingle with fellow fans. It's a pre-season opportunity to see the team and observe how they gear up for the game.

There's a dedicated area for kids with football-related activities, where young attendees can showcase their skills and learn new ones.

INDIANAPOLIS COLTS LUCAS OIL STADIUM TOURS

500 S Capitol Ave., Indianapolis
lucasoilstadium.com

For Colts fans, Lucas Oil Stadium is where the big game happens, but for families, it's a cool behind-the-scenes adventure where kids can explore one of the NFL's premier stadiums. Whether they're football-obsessed or just love big, exciting places, this tour offers a fun glimpse into what happens beyond game day.

Visitors can walk on the field, see the view from the press box, visit the locker rooms, and explore the suites like VIPs. There are plenty of great photo opportunities and sneak peeks at areas typically off-limits to the general public.

Tours last about an hour, making them just the right length for kids.

FISHERS FREIGHT FOOTBALL

Fishers Event Center, 11000 Stockdale St., Fishers
fishersfreightfootball.com

Cheering for the Fishers Freight indoor football team is a fantastic experience for families who love high-scoring games and continuous action. The team plays on a smaller field than your typical pro football team, with a smaller roster, which often leads to more touchdowns, making Freight games a hit with the younger crowd.

Attendees get a close-up view of the game, with no nosebleed seats here. Tickets are affordable for family outings, and the kids' club adds to the fun. Children especially love the mascot, Bandit the Raccoon.

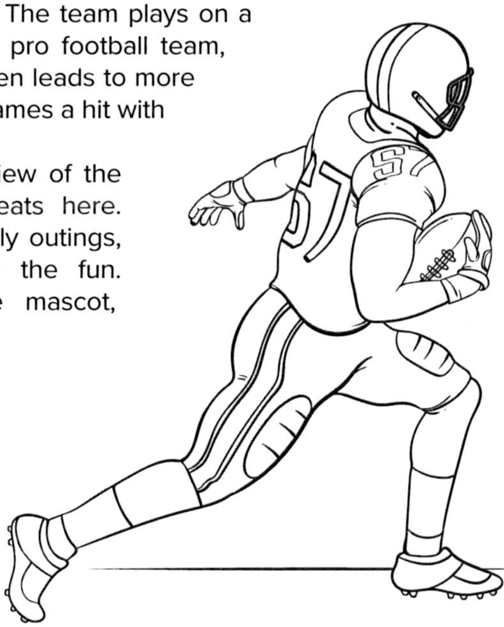

Best Spot for Hoops, Goals, and Home Runs

INDIANAPOLIS INDIANS BASEBALL

Victory Field, 501 W Maryland St., Indianapolis
milb.com/indianapolis

Catching an Indianapolis Indians game is a classic summer tradition in Indy. It's a laid-back, family-friendly outing with affordable tickets, fun for kids, a Kid Zone, between-inning entertainment, and even a special club just for young baseball fans.

Victory Field has unbeatable views of the downtown skyline, and the lawn seating area is perfect for spreading out a blanket and soaking in the sunshine while watching America's favorite summer sport.

With family perks like Kids Eat Free nights, Friday fireworks, character meet-and-greets, and themed game nights, every visit feels like a celebration.

INDIANA FEVER BASKETBALL

Gainbridge Fieldhouse,
125 S Pennsylvania St.,
Indianapolis
fever.wnba.com

The Indiana Fever is stacked with top-tier talent and rising WNBA stars. Watching a game at Gainbridge Fieldhouse is a chance to see first-class athletes compete up close. Kids love the fast pace, the games and giveaways during timeouts, and of course Freddy Fever bouncing through the stands, high-fiving fans, and keeping the energy high for everyone in the family.

Tickets start at under $20, and some deals even include a meal and team swag! It's a budget-friendly win for families who love Indiana's state sport. Arrive up to an hour early to catch pregame warm-ups and see the players before tipoff. Children under 24 months can attend for free as a lap child.

INDY ELEVEN SOCCER MATCHES

Michael A. Carroll Stadium, 1001 W New York St., Indianapolis
indyeleven.com

Indy Eleven soccer games are a go-to outing for Indianapolis-area families. With 90 minutes of fast-paced action and a quick halftime break, the matches are the perfect length for kids' shorter attention spans. Tickets are affordable, and children 3 and under get in free when seated on a parent's lap.

Gates open an hour before kickoff, giving your family plenty of time to explore the Fun Zone, where kids can win free giveaways, get their faces painted, meet the team's mascot, and enjoy other activities. After the game wraps up, many players stick around to sign autographs and snap photos with fans.

Indy Eleven fans bring serious energy; with the drumline, coordinated chants, giant flags, and team banners waving in the stands, the whole stadium is alive from start to finish.

Best Way to Visit the Past

CONNER PRAIRIE

13400 Allisonville Rd., Fishers
(317) 776-6000
connerprairie.org

Conner Prairie is the ultimate place for families who love hands-on history and outdoor adventure. This living history museum brings the past to life through costumed interpreters, historic homes, immersive exhibits, and themed festivals.

There's tons of room to run, climb, and explore—including up! Hop aboard the tethered hot air balloon and soar 350 feet into the sky as part of the 1859 Balloon Voyage. Meet historical characters, try your hand at pioneer skills, and say hello to some rare farm animals. Conner Prairie is home to one of the largest collections of heritage breeds in the US—including English Longhorn cattle, Ossabaw Island hogs, Tunis sheep, and Arapawa goats.

Events like the Headless Horseman Festival and Jupiter Flights Balloon Festival are always a sell-out, so grab your tickets early.

Credit: Tysto via Wikimedia Commons

INDIANA STATE MUSEUM

650 W Washington St., Indianapolis
(317) 232-1637
indianamuseum.org

The Indiana State Museum is a mash-up of history, science, and exhibits about the history of Indiana. Where else can kids come face-to-face with a saber-tooth cat, stand next to a giant mastodon, and explore Indiana's story from the Ice Age to the Space Age?

The museum's quirky collection of artifacts and rotating temporary exhibits keep things fresh and fun. Displays and activity areas encourage kids to touch, build, and discover, and the IMAX theater adds big-screen adventure with documentaries and special showings.

Check the calendar for exciting museum events. After your visit, stroll the nearby canal for even more fun and fresh air.

BENJAMIN HARRISON PRESIDENTIAL SITE

1230 N Delaware St., Indianapolis
(317) 631-1888
bhpsite.org

If your kids are curious about presidents or history, or just like exploring big old houses, the Benjamin Harrison Presidential Site should be on your list. Step inside the beautifully restored Victorian home of the 23rd US president, right in downtown Indy.

You'll find original furniture, personal letters, campaign posters, and even clothes that once belonged to President Harrison. Kids can peek into the kitchen, sit in the parlor, and see what life was like more than 100 years ago.

Mark your calendar for the annual Presidential Egg Roll every spring. It's just like the one at the White House, but with less travel.

Best Place to Experience Indiana's Agricultural Heritage

HUNTER'S HONEY FARM

6501 W Honey Ln., Martinsville
(765) 537-9430
huntershoneyfarm.com

Sure, bees make honey, but how? At Hunter's Honey Farm, you'll get a look at this sweet process from hive to bottle. Tours include visits to working beehives, a peek at honey extraction, and plenty of fun facts about the important role bees play in our ecosystem.

Suit up and check out a live hive, make your own beeswax candle, bottle your own honey, and of course, sample a few different varieties. Tours are available year-round, but the best time to visit is during warmer months when the bees are busiest. Reservations are recommended.

FISHERS AGRIPARK

11171 Florida Rd., Fishers
(317) 595-3150
fishersagripark.com

If digging in the dirt, seeing animals, and growing things sound like fun, Fishers AgriPark is waiting for you. This 33-acre working farm is full of crops to explore, farm animals to meet, and nature-based play that keeps kids excited to come back.

Stroll through rows of corn, tomatoes, sunflowers, and pumpkins. During the growing season, families can even pick fresh produce straight from the fields to take home.

Little ones love the nature-inspired playground, with balance features, climbing elements, and a mud kitchen perfect for cooking up imaginary meals. The park is open seasonally from May through October, and it's completely free to visit. Just check the hours before you go.

INDIANA STATE FAIR

1202 E 38th St., Indianapolis
indianastatefair.com

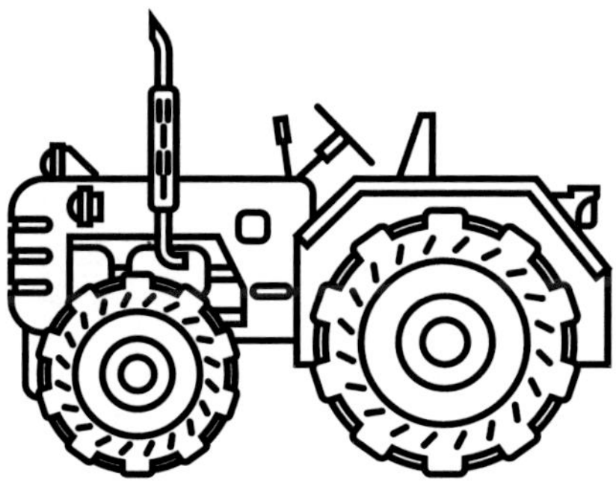

Everyone knows the Indiana State Fair is packed with rides and deep-fried everything, but it's also a fun, hands-on way for kids to learn about farming, animals, and where our food comes from. If your crew loves tractors, baby animals, or getting a little dirty, this is the place to be.

Wander through the livestock barns to meet cows, pigs, goats, and more. Some of them are just days old! Watch 4-H kids care for their animals or chat with a real farmer in the Glass Barn. Try your skills on a combine simulator or let your littles get to work at Little Hands on the Farm, where they'll experience life on a pretend farm.

Don't forget to treat yourselves to a milkshake at the famous Dairy Bar on your way out.

Best Place to Learn about Animals

NINE LIVES CAT CAFÉ

1315 Shelby St., Indianapolis
(317) 602-5287
ninelivescatcafe.com

Central Indiana is home to a paw-full lot of cat cafés, and each has a mission to improve the lives of feline friends. If your kids love cats and you're looking for a purrfect outing, Nine Lives Cat Café is it.

Order a latte or hot cocoa, then head into the Cat Lounge where friendly felines roam freely, ready for pets, playtime, or snuggles. Kids love the tactile experience, and you just might find your next furry family member.

Reservations are recommended, and there's a small entry fee that helps cover the cats' care.

PRANCING PONIES

17873 Joliet Rd., Sheridan
(317) 514-7720

Miniature ponies are adorable on TikTok, but they're even better in real life! Prancing Ponies is a charming, family-run farm where kids can enjoy pony rides and meet friendly farm animals.

Each summer, they host Unlimited Pony Ride Fridays. Your little cowboy or cowgirl can ride as many times as they want for a small fee. Prancing Ponies is home to a donkey, sheep, goats, chickens, and bunnies, giving kids plenty of opportunities to meet and learn about friendly farm animals. They also offer seasonal farm camps and their famous holiday "pony-grams."

OINKING ACRES FARM RESCUE & SANCTUARY

8420 N County Rd. 650 E, Brownsburg
(317) 225-1761
oinkingacres.org

Oinking Acres Farm Rescue & Sanctuary provides a safe home for pigs, cows, goats, sheep, donkeys, mini-horses, mules, and other farmyard creatures, giving visitors a chance to meet and learn about the animals. The pigs, from tiny piglets to full-grown pot-bellied pigs, are how it all started.

Kids can watch the animals roam, nap, root around in the dirt, eat, and play, all while learning about animal rescue and why so many end up at sanctuaries like this one. The experience is up close, personal, and unforgettable.

Self-guided tours are available for a small fee; check the website for hours. Please leave strollers and wagons at home.

Best Place for Kids Who Love Trains

INDIANA LIVE STEAMERS AT JOHNSON COUNTY PARK

3008 Rodeo Dr., Franklin
indianalivesteamers.org

You can take a real train ride on a miniature railroad through Johnson County Park. These 7.5-inch gauge trains are just the right size for passengers and take families on a 20-minute journey through the woods, across bridges, and past a train station replica.

The ride is packed with fun details; working signals, friendly conductors, and scenic tracks make it a favorite for train-loving kids. There's a small fee to ride, and trains operate only a few times each year for the public. The railroad engineers are great at connecting with young train fans.

Closed-toe shoes are required, so plan accordingly. Visit the website for dates and times.

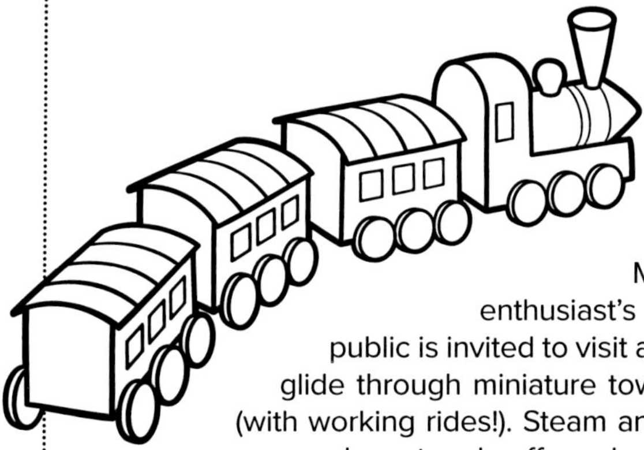

MR. MUFFIN'S TRAINS

165 E Main St., Atlanta
(765) 292-2022
mrmuffinstrains.com

Mr. Muffin's Trains is a train enthusiast's dream. Most Saturdays, the public is invited to visit and watch O-gauge model trains glide through miniature towns, farms, and carnival scenes (with working rides!). Steam and diesel engines crisscross the enormous layout and puff overhead across bridges.

Steve and Liz Nelson, aka Mr. and Mrs. Muffin, have poured their hearts into this breathtaking shop. Say hi when you stop by for train sets, collector's items, and everything your railfan could ever want.

PIZZA KING STATION

7045 Bluff Rd., Indianapolis
(317) 883-0777

8100 E US Hwy. 36, Avon
(317) 272-1707

theoriginalpizzaking.com

Pizza and trains: can you name a better combo? At Pizza King Station, your drinks arrive via a miniature train that travels through the restaurant on a track system right to your table.

The booths are designed to look like train cars, and in some locations, you'll order using a retro intercom system. Kids love waiting for the little train to make a stop at their table with their soda or chocolate milk, and then waving goodbye until the next round.

The menu features kid-friendly items like thin-crust pizza, sandwiches, and pasta.

Best Spot for Aviation Adventures

FIRST WING JET CENTER OPEN HOUSE

Indianapolis Executive Airport,
11329 E State Rd. 32, Zionsville
(317) 769-4487
wingsoverindy.com

The annual Open House at the First Wing Jet Center is a well-loved fly-in event that doubles as a fundraiser for Down Syndrome Indiana. Families can be just steps away from all kinds of aircraft: vintage warbirds, modern jets, and even stunt aircraft.

There are takeoffs, landings, and airplane rides throughout the day. Kids love the educational booths, flight demos, and always-popular airplane candy drop. Food trucks and activities keep the whole family entertained.

Admission is free, but donations are encouraged and support a great cause. The open house is traditionally held in June.

vintage warbirds, modern jets, and even stunt aircraft

AIRPORT DAY

Indy South Greenwood Airport, 897 Airport Pkwy., Greenwood
(317) 881-0887
greenwood.in.gov/department/index.php?structureid=37

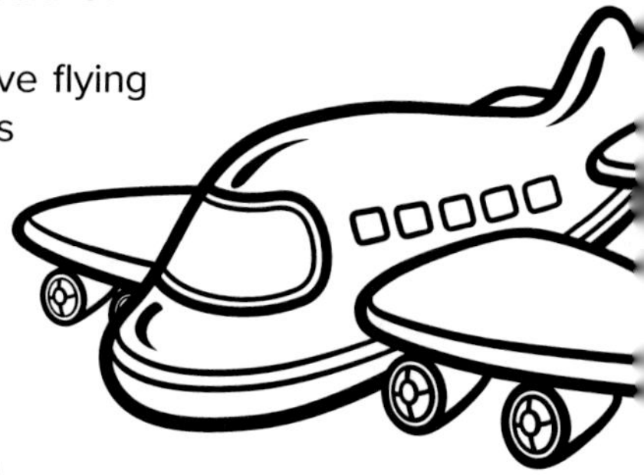

Airport Day is "just plane fun" for kids who love flying and aircraft. Airplanes, helicopters, and all things aviation are featured at the annual family-friendly aviation festival. Each summer, guests can get a rare look at aircraft from just a few feet away, meet real pilots, and even take a flight.

Kids ages 8–17 can even take a free ride through the Young Eagles program (registration required in advance). Check out flight simulators, vintage warbirds, military aircraft, and food trucks. Visit the website for dates; typically Airport Day is at the end of August.

RADIO CONTROLLED AIRCRAFT FLY-INS

Johnson County Radio Control Flyers
Tracee Field, 2949 North St., Nineveh
jcrcf.wordpress.com

Northeast Side Taildraggers R/C Aviation Club (NeST)
12896 E 166th St., Noblesville
nest-rc.org

Who says only full-size aircraft are exciting? R/C (radio-controlled) fly-ins are a blast for families who want to experience aviation on a smaller scale. Watch skilled hobbyists pilot high-speed jets, stunt planes, and scale-model warbirds through loops, dives, and sky-high tricks.

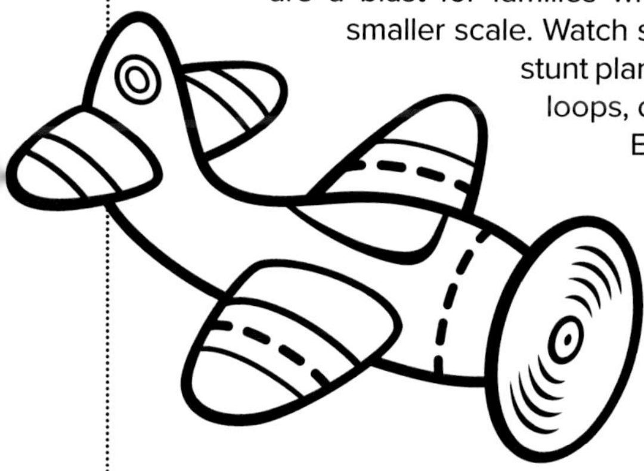

Events are held several times a year and are usually free to attend. Bring lawn chairs, sunscreen, and sunglasses. You'll be amazed at what these tiny planes can do and the real-life details that are captured in miniature form.

Best Place to See Classic Cars and Racing Legends

INDIANAPOLIS MOTOR SPEEDWAY MUSEUM

4750 W 16th St., Indianapolis
(317) 492-6784
imsmuseum.org

The Indianapolis Motor Speedway Museum is the ultimate destination for everything about cars, speed, and automotive racing history. Located inside the world-famous Indianapolis Motor Speedway, there's no better place to see Indy 500-winning cars and exhibits that showcase the evolution of racing.

Kids will love getting up close to the sleek race cars and seeing how design and technology have changed over the years. Interactive displays and eye-catching motorsport-themed artwork make it a fun visit for the whole family.

Don't miss the Kiss the Bricks Tour, where you'll hop on a bus, cruise around the track, and finish with a chance to kneel down and kiss the famous Yard of Bricks, just like the Indy 500 champs.

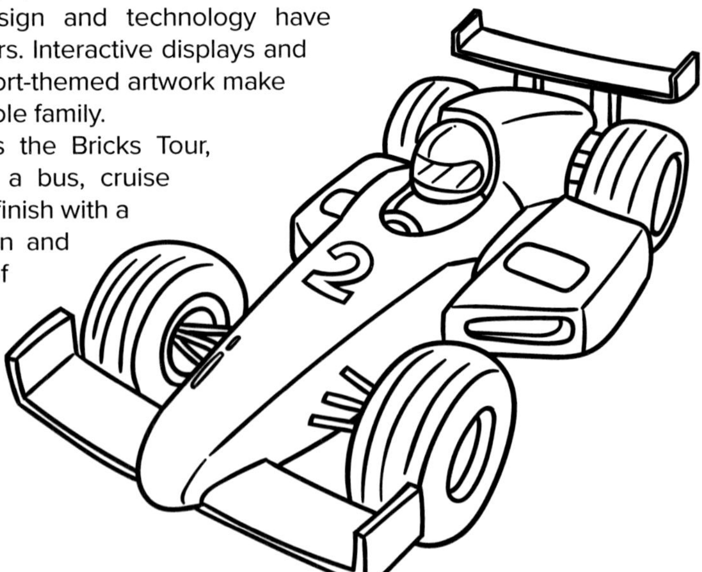

INDIANAPOLIS CARS & COFFEE

Various locations around Indianapolis
indianapoliscarsandcoffee.org

If your kids can name more car brands than candy bars, Indianapolis Cars & Coffee is your new Saturday morning stop. This free, family-friendly event brings out a collection of muscle cars, luxury rides, and decked-out sports cars. Car owners are happy to chat, so kids can ask questions, peek under hoods, and learn what makes each car unique.

Events are held on select Saturday mornings throughout Central Indiana at rotating locations, from dealerships to museums to racetracks; you never know where Cars & Coffee will pop up. It's casual, and yes, there's coffee for the grown-ups. Check the website for the current schedule and location lineup.

THE STUTZ CAR MUSEUM

1060 N Capitol Ave., Indianapolis
(317) 488-7374
thestutz.com

The legacy of the Stutz Motor Car Company, known for luxury and speed in the early 1900s, lives on at the historic Stutz Building in downtown Indianapolis. Families can stop by the Stutz Car Museum for a free visit and get a look at vintage cars while learning about American auto history.

The building itself was once home to the Stutz factory, so it's the natural place to see beautifully restored vehicles, including the legendary Stutz Bearcat, one of the coolest sports cars of its time. It's a quick and easy stop downtown; the museum is open on select days, so check their website or give them a call before your visit.

Best Way to Experience Indy's Racing Spirit

500 FESTIVAL EVENTS

Various locations in Indianapolis
500festival.com

The 500 Festival is all about celebrating the Indy 500 all month long, with fun that happens off the track. Families can join in a parade, fun runs, and hands-on activities leading up to the big race.

Don't miss the 500 Festival Parade, packed with giant floats, marching bands, race car drivers, and pure race-day energy. The Mini-Marathon includes both a 5K and half-marathon, with lots of kids training through the KidsFit Program.

Kids' Day and the Rookie Run are a favorite for young fans. For one day, Monument Circle transforms into a free downtown festival with bounce houses, games, crafts, and race-themed fun just for kids.

LUCAS OIL INDIANAPOLIS RACEWAY PARK

10267 US Hwy. 136, Indianapolis
raceirp.com

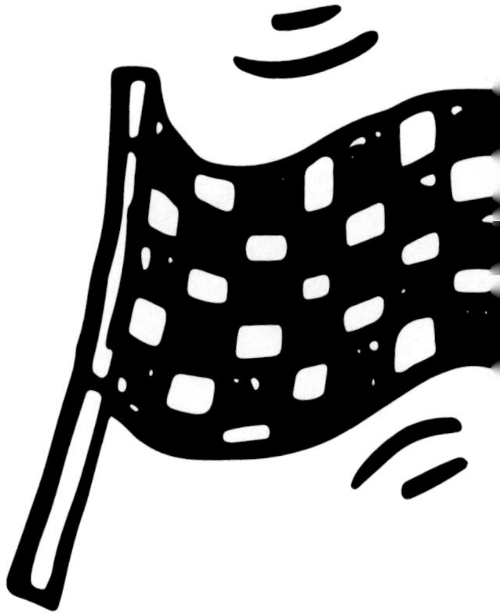

Lucas Oil Raceway is where families go for edge-of-your-seat, adrenaline-pumping fun. With both a drag strip and oval track, the venue hosts NHRA drag racing, stock car events, and a variety of high-speed events.

The NHRA US Nationals, held every Labor Day weekend, are a must-see. Kids can watch as cars reach over 300 mph in just seconds. You can literally feel the engines rumble through your body! Flames shoot from exhaust pipes, tires smoke, and excitement fills the air as the cars rocket down the strip.

At many events, pit passes give you access to the cars, garages, and even the drivers. Don't forget ear protection and sunscreen.

INDIANAPOLIS MOTOR SPEEDWAY

4790 W 16th St., Indianapolis
indianapolismotorspeedway.com

There's no question that the Indianapolis Motor Speedway is the best place on Earth for high-speed family fun. Fast cars, roaring engines, and the thrill of the track are practically a rite of passage for Indy kids. As the home of the world-famous Indianapolis 500, the speedway hosts racing events all year long.

Kids can attend any number of races, from the Grand Prix to NASCAR and beyond. However, IndyCar Test Days and practice sessions are a great way to have a high-octane experience without the crowds. Many of the races have kid zones, driver meet-and-greets, and entertainment. Tickets vary by event, but kids 15 and under are often free with a paying adult.

Best Spot for Curious Minds and Unexpected Finds

WORLD'S LARGEST BALL OF PAINT

10696 N 200 W, Alexandria
(765) 724-4088

A visit to the World's Largest Ball of Paint in Alexandria, Indiana, is a must. This roadside treasure started in 1977 when Michael Carmichael and his son painted a baseball. Today, it's an enormous sphere covered in tens of thousands of layers of paint weighing in at over 10,000 pounds.

Call ahead to make a free appointment (donations accepted) to add your own layer of paint, and since this is a Guinness World Record holder, your kids will be part of the record. Your kids will choose a color, grab a roller or brush, and leave their mark. Every painter gets a certificate to remember their contribution.

tens of thousands of layers of paint weighing in at over 10,000 pounds

MUSEUM OF MINIATURE HOUSES & OTHER COLLECTIONS

111 E Main St., Carmel
(317) 575-9466
museumofminiatures.org

Step into a world where everything is teeny-tiny at the Museum of Miniature Houses. This museum is packed with beautifully detailed dollhouses, miniature homes, room displays, and everyday scenes shrunk down to scale. If your kids love miniatures and imaginative play, this place is a treat.

Grab a magnifying glass, climb up on a step stool, and go on a scavenger hunt through tiny kitchens, living rooms, and fairy-tale settings. There's even a dollhouse you can play with and a wishing fairy door. Audio tours are available, and special events take place several times a year.

INDIANA MEDICAL HISTORY MUSEUM

3270 Kirkbride Way, Indianapolis
(317) 635-7329
imhm.org

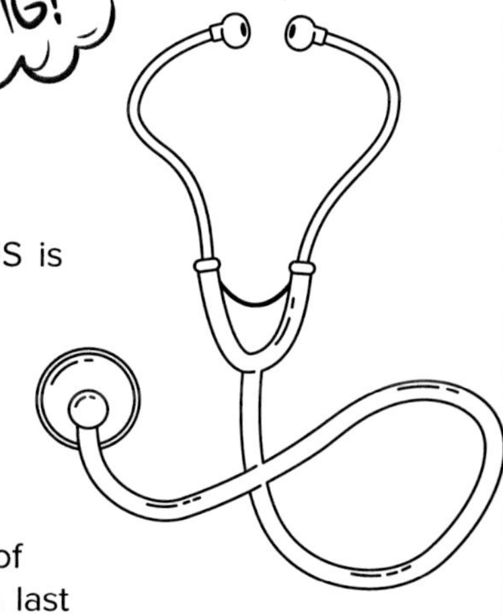

The oldest surviving pathology building in the US is home to the Indiana Medical History Museum. Kids who like oddities, history, and the wonders of medical science will appreciate a visit here.

You'll tour a preserved 1950s doctor's office; visit an old-school autopsy room; and see fascinating, and sometimes a little spooky, medical artifacts. There are real brains on display as part of the preserved specimen collection! Guided tours last about an hour and must be booked in advance.

The museum is best suited for older kids and teens who are comfortable with scientific topics as some exhibits, like preserved organs and discussions about sensitive medical treatments, may not be ideal for younger children.

Best Quirky Attraction

CIRCUS CAPITAL OF THE WORLD: PERU, INDIANA

Various locations in Peru

The magic of the circus lives on in Peru, Indiana—daring acrobats, gallant elephants, and silly clowns. They're all part of the events and attractions in Peru.

At the International Circus Hall of Fame (3076 E Circus Ln.), you can explore vintage circus wagons, posters, and costumes on the historic grounds once used by the Wallace Circus. Nearby, the Circus City Museum (154 N Broadway) showcases colorful costumes, photos, and miniatures that tell the town's circus story.

Each July, the Peru Amateur Circus (154 N Broadway) takes center stage for eight days of performances by locals ages 7 to 21. Add in carnival rides, a circus parade, and plenty of fair food, and you've got a full day of big top fun.

ANTIQUE FAN MUSEUM

10983 Bennett Pkwy., Zionsville
(317) 733-4113
fanimation.com/museum

If your kid is a fan of quirky, one-of-a-kind museums, the Antique Fan Museum in Zionsville will blow them away—literally! You'll see over 2,000 antique fans from around the world, some dating back to the 1880s, everything from early steam-powered and battery-operated fans to hand-cranked and belt-driven models.

The museum, located inside Fanimation, a working fan company, is open by appointment only. There's a small fee for admission.

WHO NORTH AMERICA

8901 S State Rd. 67, Camby
(317) 481-8189
whona.com

Time travel and sci-fi adventures await at Who North America, the only museum and retail space in the world dedicated entirely to Doctor Who. Inside, you'll find props, toys, collectibles, and memorabilia from every era of the iconic British series.

Snap a photo with the full-size TARDIS, play a round on the Doctor Who pinball machine, and browse shelves full of merchandise that spans galaxies. Whether you're introducing your kids to the Doctor or geeking out as a lifelong fan, there's something for everyone here. Admission is free, but don't be surprised if a few treasures follow you home.

Best Place to See the Stars

CARMEL HIGH SCHOOL PLANETARIUM

520 E Main St., Carmel
ccs.k12.in.us/chs/academics/planetarium

The Carmel High School Planetarium has an engaging and educational show that's perfect for budding astronomers. Located within Carmel High School, this planetarium regularly opens its doors to the public for family-friendly astronomy shows. Each 40-minute show features a different theme, exploring questions in modern astronomy, bringing the night sky to life, and taking visitors on a journey beyond Earth.

On clear nights, student volunteers often set up telescopes for a bonus peek at the real night sky. Ticket prices are budget-friendly, with discounted rates for students and kids.

STARGAZING AT MCCLOUD NATURE PARK

8518 Hughes Rd., North Salem
hendrickscountyparks.org

Ready to get outside at night and explore the stars? The Indiana Astronomical Society partners with Hendricks County Parks & Recreation to hold free sky seminars and viewings away from city lights. During these seasonal events, guests have free access to telescopes of various sizes, allowing both children and adults to view planets, stars, and other cosmic wonders.

Each event kicks off with a 30-minute talk inside the Nature Center, covering what constellations and planets to watch for. Then, head outside to view the night sky through high-powered telescopes. You might see Saturn's rings, star clusters, or even a passing comet! Stargazing is family-friendly, but the seminars are best for kids ages 8 and up.

HOLCOMB OBSERVATORY AND PLANETARIUM

4600 Sunset Ave., Indianapolis
(317) 940-8333
butler.edu/observatory

If your kids love stars, planets, and the vast universe, the Holcomb Observatory and Planetarium at Butler University is the perfect place to explore the stars. The giant 38-inch Cassegrain reflector telescope, one of the largest public telescopes in the US, gives visitors a rare opportunity to take a peek at the moon, planets, and distant galaxies in breathtaking detail.

Inside the planetarium, families can watch a show about space, exploring constellations, planets, and cosmic phenomena. On clear nights, visitors can view the night sky through the powerful telescope, spotting treasures like the rings of Saturn or the craters on the Moon. There is an admission fee, and reservations are suggested.

Best Place for High Tech Fun

RUPERT'S ARCADE

109 S Harrison St., Shelbyville
(317) 654-5682
rupertsarcade.com

If your kids are arcade lovers, Rupert's Arcade has a mix of classic and modern arcade games, all available for unlimited play with the purchase of admission.

Founded by *Survivor* fan favorite Rupert Boneham, this arcade helps support Rupert's Kids, a nonprofit empowering youth and adults to find purpose and confidence. Whether you're introducing your kids to your favorite childhood games or looking for an affordable family outing, this is a win-win experience.

PINS MECHANICAL CO.

856 Carrollton Ave., Indianapolis
(463) 600-9100
pinsbar.com/locations/indianapolis

Any time is a great time to visit Pins Mechanical Co., but when the weather's nice, the outdoor patio, with yard games and a fire pit, is extra awesome. Inside, you'll find old-school fun like duckpin bowling, pinball, and foosball.

Located in the Bottleworks District, Pins Mechanical is perfect for families during the day (before 9 p.m., when it becomes 21+). Try Giant Jenga, Connect Four, and other favorites, then grab a bite from the Garage Food Hall or catch a movie at the Living Room Lounge. You can even keep the fun going at Sandbox VR, just steps away!

SANDBOX VR

850 Massachusetts Ave., Suite 150, Indianapolis
(317) 999-9908
sandboxvr.com/indianapolis

Kids who love gaming or adventure stories will love Sandbox VR. It's a virtual reality experience that drops you right into the action as you step into a video game.

Families (older kids, teens, and grown-ups) can team up and explore virtual worlds together, fending off zombies, exploring outer space, or battling robots in a futuristic city. Participants wear high-tech VR headsets and a special vest that has haptic feedback so you can feel the vibrations of explosions, hear everything in surround sound, and move freely with your group. The games are fast-paced, intense, and incredibly realistic and last around 30 minutes.

Best Table-Top Game Hangout

PARADIGM GAMES

2479 N Meridian St., Indianapolis
(715) 379-6831
facebook.com/paradigmgamesllc

Paradigm Games is a great spot for families looking to try new games or level up their hobby. From Magic: The Gathering to Pokémon and Dungeons & Dragons, there's always something happening here. Both casual and serious gamers are welcome to stop in for tournaments, events, and group game-play.

Browse new and gently used board and card games, or borrow a title from the Board Game Library and try before you buy. Bonus: they buy collectible games and cards too—so you might just trade your way into something new!

FAMILY TIME GAMES

8796 Michigan Rd., Indianapolis
(317) 429-9817
shop.family-time-games.com

Family Time Games is host to various events for a wide variety of gaming enthusiasts. Game nights, tournaments for board games, card games, role-playing games, and miniature tabletop strategy games: Family Time Games is all about play.

With more than 25 tables and an impressive game library, you can test out dozens of games before deciding which ones to bring home. It's a welcoming space to discover new favorites, play as a family, and connect with others who love games.

MOONSHOT GAMES

50 N Ninth St., Noblesville
(317) 662-2889
moonshotgamestore.com

Moonshot is the ultimate spot for board games, card games, minis, paints, and Dungeons & Dragons. Game players gather from all over Central Indiana to meet up for tournaments and releases.

Throughout the week, you'll find scheduled game nights and workshops—including friendly learn-to-play events where kids and their grown-ups can discover new games without pressure. During school breaks, check out Moonshot's themed mini camps for young gamers. The staff are pros at helping families find the perfect game for every age and interest.

Best Only-in-Indiana Experience

Credit: Sarah Stierch via Wikimedia Commons

SLEEP IN A TRAIN CAR HOTEL ROOM

Crowne Plaza Indianapolis Downtown Union Station
123 W Louisiana St., Indianapolis
(317) 631-2221
ihg.com

Kids will love an overnight stay at the Crowne Plaza at Union Station, where you can sleep in a real 1920s Pullman train car. These 26 train car rooms sit on the original tracks inside America's first Union Station, and yes, they're still inside the building!

Each car is named after a notable figure from the early 1900s and features a cozy room, perfect for families of up to four people. Even the hotel pool is set inside the historic train shed, which adds to the experience for train-loving kids (and grown-ups).

FEAST OF LANTERNS AT SPADES PARK

1800 Nowland Ave., Indianapolis
indyfol.org

Each August, Spades Park lights up for the Feast of Lanterns, a neighborhood tradition that began in the 1800s and is now beloved by the whole city. Families spread out blankets and picnic under hundreds of colorful lanterns strung through the trees. Children play on the playground, make crafts, and rule the Kid Zone, and everyone dances to the live music from local bands.

All evening, food trucks serve up snacks, beverages, and meals, while artists and vendors have their products for sale. As dusk turns to night, the magic hits as the colorful lanterns light up the sky, creating a beautiful summer scene. Admission is free, so bring along a blanket or chairs and get ready to fall in love with this community event.

ROCK-COLA 50'S CAFE

5730 S Brookville Rd., Indianapolis
(317) 357-2233
rock-cola-50s-cafe.foodjoyy.com

Back in the 1940s, Choc-Ola, a rich, chocolatey beverage, was born in Indianapolis and quickly became a local favorite. Now, it's making a nostalgic comeback, and there's no better place to sip it than inside a real 1950s diner.

Rock-Cola 50's Cafe is a step back in time, complete with counter service, retro decor, and colorful vintage memorabilia lining the walls. Kids love the bright colors, the cozy booths, and the food. Stop in for a classic American meal of burgers, sandwiches, hearty breakfasts, and of course, a cold can of Choc-Ola. Hours vary, so be sure to check before your visit.

Best Place to Splash Around

WEST PARK SPLASH PAD

2700 W 116th St., Carmel
carmelclayparks.com

West Park has a splash pad that blends natural elements with water play. Kids can slosh through a canyon-like creek and puddle jump beneath gentle waterfalls. Open seasonally from Memorial Day through September, the West Park splash pad is great for cooling off on a hot day.

In addition to the splash pad, there's a two-story playground with extra-long slides and climbing poles that challenge older kids, while little ones enjoy a separate play space with swings, interactive musical features, and smaller slides. Families can also explore the nature playground, more than two miles of scenic trails, a prairie maze, fishing areas, and shaded picnic spots. In the winter, Jill's Hill becomes one of the best sledding spots in Carmel—bring your sled!

MULBERRY FIELDS SPLASH PAD

9645 Whitestown Rd., Zionsville
zionsville-in.gov

One of the most unique splash pads in Central Indiana can be found at Mulberry Fields in Zionsville. Instead of traditional fountains and sprayers, this water play area features a winding, man-made creek with smooth rocks; shallow pools; and gentle, trickling waterfalls. It's the perfect spot for kids who love to splash, explore, and cool off while pretending they're creek explorers.

The splash pad operates during the warmer months, but the park is open year-round. Amenities include a large playground, restrooms, picnic shelters, open green spaces, paved trails, a skate park, and pickleball courts. There's even a big hill where the community goes sledding in the winter.

WATERMILL SPLASH PAD AT WILLIAMS PARK

940 S Locust Ln., Brownsburg
brownsburgparks.com

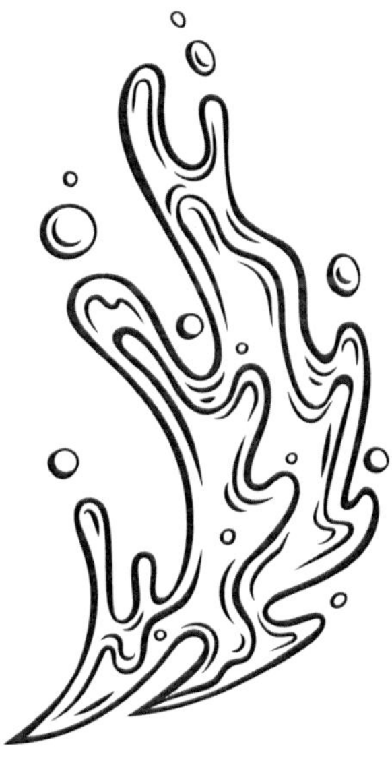

The Watermill Splash Pad at Williams Park is a summertime favorite in Brownsburg. The splash pad has plenty of water elements: misting sprayers, darting water jets, and spinning features. Bigger kids gravitate toward the water cannons and action-packed elements, while toddlers enjoy gentler sprays in the mellow, tot-friendly section.

Across the park from the splash pad is the epic wooden Blast Off Playground, a towering, maze-like structure full of tunnels, towers, and hiding spots that spark hours of imaginative play. Families also love the park's paved trails, shaded picnic shelters, butterfly garden, basketball courts, and open green spaces perfect for running wild or relaxing in the sun.

Best Place to Enjoy Water Sports

FRANK'S PADDLESPORTS LIVERY

3001 N White River Pkwy. Dr. W, Indianapolis
(260) 226-3075
frankslivery.com

Frank's Paddlesports Livery is your one-stop place for a family-friendly water adventure. If you want to try canoeing, kayaking, or stand-up paddleboarding, they have everything you need, right along the scenic White River across from Riverside Park.

Choose from a relaxing paddle on your own or join a guided trip. There's a four-mile or seven-mile route. The staff gets you geared up and drops you off upriver, and then it's just you, the kids, the water, and the typical Indiana wildlife sighting. Keep an eye out for turtles, birds, and other local wildlife as you float along. Kids love the adventure, and no matter your experience level, this is a great way to enjoy the outdoors and your city. Reservations are recommended.

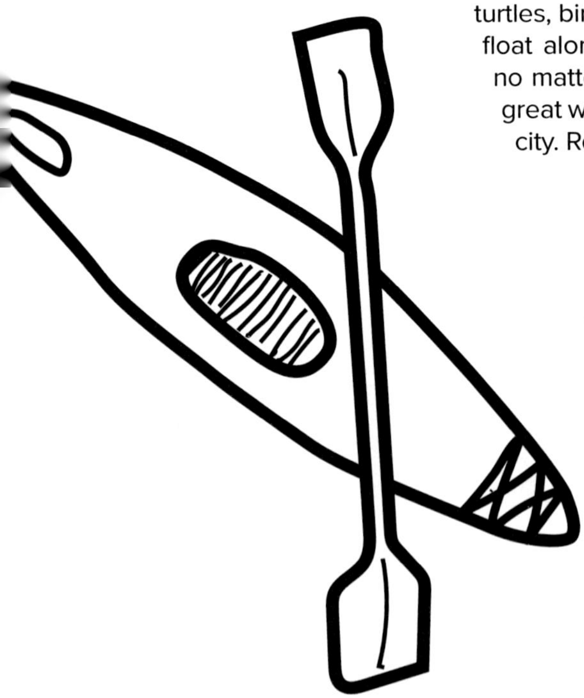

WHEEL FUN RENTALS

White River State Park & Canal: 801 W Washington St., Indianapolis
Geist Waterfront: 10811 Olio Rd., Fishers
Eagle Creek Park: 7840 W 56th St., Indianapolis
wheelfunrentals.com

Locals and visitors alike appreciate the fun, active ways Wheel Fun Rentals helps families explore Indy, on land and on water. At the Indianapolis Canal, you can hop into a swan pedal boat or kayak for a laid-back paddle through the city with skyline views all around. A little farther down at White River State Park, trade the water for wheels and cruise the trails on a surrey, a chopper bicycle, a cruiser, a tandem bike, or even an electric bike. It's a fun way to cover more ground while still keeping it relaxed.

At Eagle Creek Park, there are kayaks, pedal boats, pontoon boats, stand-up paddleboards, canoes, and bike rentals available so your family can explore. Planning a visit to Geist Waterfront Park? You can rent kayaks and stand-up paddleboards while you're there.

MORSE MARINA

20999 Hague Rd., Noblesville
(317) 984-3301
morsemarina.com

If your family's idea of fun includes a day on the water, Morse Marina is a go-to spot for a laid-back lake adventure on Morse Reservoir. You can rent a pontoon that seats up to 10 people and spend the day cruising, swimming, fishing, or just soaking up the sun. Even if you've never boated before, the rental process is simple and beginner-friendly.

Pack a cooler with lunch and drinks, or make a stop at one of the lakeside restaurants. Dock at Wolfies Waterfront Grill, a casual, family-friendly favorite, or head to the north end of the reservoir for a meal at the BoatHouse Kitchen & Swan Dive. It's the kind of easy summer outing everyone will remember.

Best Place to Tube Down the River

WHITE RIVER CANOE COMPANY

17180 River Rd., Noblesville
(317) 867-4233
whiterivercanoe.com

Riding an inner tube down the river with your kids is the kind of unplugged, laugh-out-loud fun they'll be talking about all summer. Whether you want to float for a couple of hours or the whole afternoon, White River Canoe Company will hook you up with everything you need for a relaxing tubing trip on the White River.

Pack a lunch, toss some drinks in a small cooler, and don't skimp on the sunscreen. After a quick shuttle ride to your launch spot, you'll hop into your tube and spend the day drifting downstream. Eat your lunch as you float, or pull off on a quiet embankment for a riverside picnic. Keep an eye out for turtles, herons, and other river wildlife, but don't forget to tether your tubes! You'll exit the water where your car is parked. Reservations are recommended.

SUGAR VALLEY CANOE TRIPS

1313 IN 47, Marshall
(765) 597-2364
sugarvalleycanoes.com

A tubing adventure at Turkey Run is a classic Midwest activity. It's just you, your kids, and the slow-moving current carrying you past sandstone cliffs, shady trees, and historic covered bridges. Add a few splash fights and some toe-dipping breaks, and it's the quintessential summer day.

Sugar Valley Canoe Trips provides everything you need, including a shuttle to your starting point and all the gear. The three-mile float takes about two to three hours. Cooler tubes are available for rent so your snacks and drinks can come along for the ride. Don't forget water shoes, sunscreen, and plenty of drinking water.

MORGAN'S OUTDOOR ADVENTURES

7040 Whitewater River Ln., Brookville
(765) 647-4904
morganscanoe.com

Morgan's Outdoor Adventures in Brookville is a favorite for tubing and river fun just about an hour from Indianapolis. Kids will love floating in their own tubes or linking up with yours, spotting turtles on the shore, and dipping their toes in the cool water.

The Brookville livery takes you to the drop-in point along the Whitewater River. From there, it's a five-mile float back to their lodge. Sit back and enjoy the gentle current as it carries you through tree-lined scenery and open water.

Want more than just tubing? They also offer raft, kayak, and canoe rentals. Stay for the weekend with riverside camping or cabins. Reservations are required, and weekends book quickly.

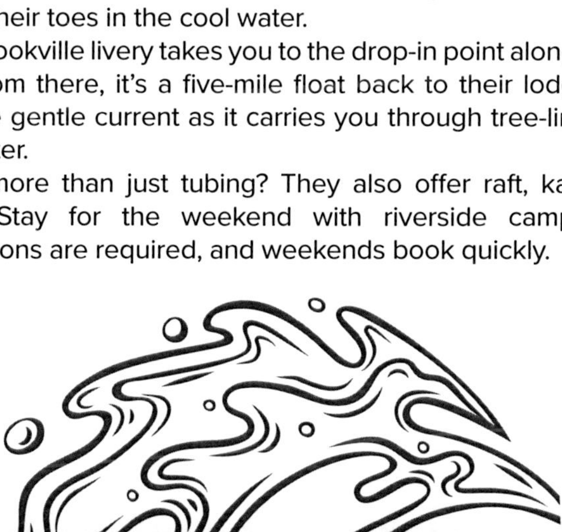

Best Spot for a Day on the Beach

MONROE LAKE

4850 S State Rd. 446, Bloomington
(812) 837-9546
dnr.in.gov

From Memorial Day to Labor Day, Monroe Lake is where families go for beach days and lake adventures. Dip those feet in the water or get some sun at one of three public beaches: Fairfax, Paynetown, and Hardin Ridge State Recreation Areas.

Fairfax has a swimming beach, picnic areas, and boat ramps, and it is home to Fourwinds Lakeside Inn & Marina, a great spot to rent boats for waterskiing, knee-boarding, and inner tubing. Paynetown has a quiet swimming beach, while Hardin Ridge has a beach, shelter, and shower house along with campsites.

Pack a lunch; wear your swimsuits; and bring a kite, Frisbee, and sand toys. Many families enjoy camping in this area and creating a weekend of outdoor fun at Indiana's largest reservoir.

EAGLE CREEK PARK BEACH

7602 Eagle Beach Dr., Indianapolis
parks.indy.gov

Eagle Creek Park Beach is a tucked-away sandy spot along the reservoir that's perfect for cooling off in the summer. A designated roped-off swimming area makes it safe for wading and splashing, and lifeguards are on duty during posted hours. There's plenty of space to spread out towels or set up beach chairs.

The lake water can be a little murky, so if swimming isn't your thing, bring buckets and shovels and enjoy some beach play with your kids.

Bring snacks, sun protection, and a chair or two. There's a small admission fee, or you can purchase an annual pass.

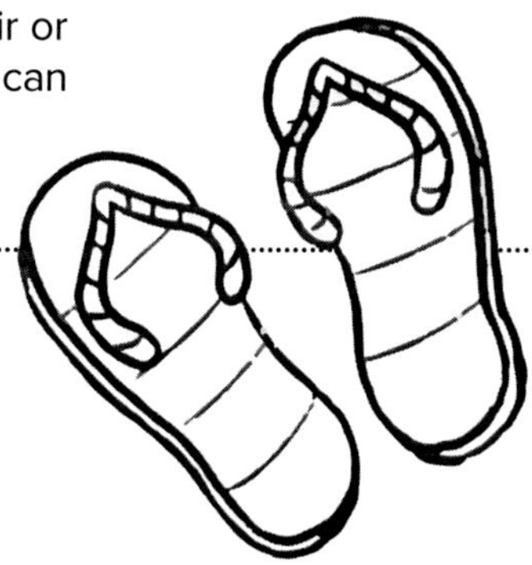

GEIST WATERFRONT PARK

10811 Olio Rd., Fishers
playfishers.com

Geist Waterfront Park is a scenic spot located on the shore of Geist Reservoir. It's a great place for a summer outing. The beach has soft, fine sand great for spreading out blankets, building castles, or dipping toes in the water. After your beach play, there's a rinse-off shower to freshen up.

Arguably, the best part of a visit to Geist Waterfront Park is the pirate-themed playground. Kids will pretend to set sail on the high seas, climbing, sliding, and playing in the shaded sand and water play areas, perfect for little ones not quite ready for big lake adventures.

Park access is free for everyone during non-peak hours, however during peak hours there is a parking fee for non-Fishers residents.

Best Destination for Warm Weather Fun

FREEDOM SPRINGS AQUATICS PARK

850 W Stop 18 Rd., Greenwood
(317) 884-2078
greenwood.in.gov/freedomsprings

Freedom Springs is where families head to beat the heat on the south side of Indy. This aquatics park has it all: towering slides, diving boards, a lazy river, and a dedicated toddler splash area.

Race down the two body slides, grab a buddy for the tube slide, and hang on tight for the high-speed drop slide. Prefer a slower pace? Drift along the lazy river while the kids take on the lily pad crossing challenge.

Cabanas and shelters are available to rent for a half or full day. Greenwood residents, military members, and veterans receive admission discounts.

THE WATERPARK AT THE MONON COMMUNITY CENTER

1195 Central Park Dr. W, Carmel
(317) 848-7275
carmelclayparks.com/the-waterpark

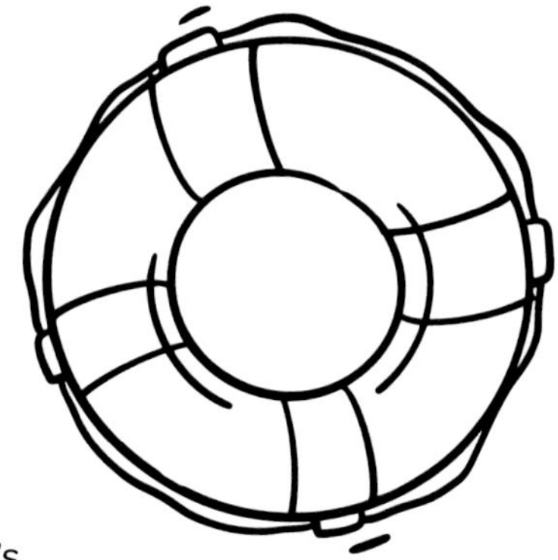

The Waterpark at the Monon Community Center is a must-visit for summer fun. Adults, you'll love relaxing as you drift along the lazy river. Everyone can test their skills on the FlowRider, a surfing simulator that's part wave, part wipeout. The water slides are thrilling and a hit with all ages.

There's a zero-depth entry water play area with sprayers, dumping buckets, and mini slides. Younger kids can splash in the separate kiddie pool and activity area that's designed just for them.

Bring your own lunch or grab treats from the concession stand. Admission fees apply, but Monon Community Center members get in free.

SPLASH ISLAND FAMILY WATERPARK

651 Vestal Rd., Plainfield
(317) 839-7665
plainfieldparks.com/splash-island

Splash Island in Plainfield is a 4.5-acre Caribbean-themed waterpark with something for everyone. There are six unique water slides, a winding leisure river, a six-lane lap pool with diving boards, and tons of splash zones. Open from Memorial Day weekend through Labor Day, it's a summer favorite for good reason.

Families with young children love the multiple play areas just for littles, including the splash pad and the kiddie pool with mini slides.

During the colder months or if you just want to play indoors, the Richard A. Carlucci Recreation and Aquatic Center is home to a small indoor waterpark. There's a zero-depth entry pool, water slide, and other interactive water features.

Best Outdoor Swimming Pool

SPLASH HOUSE WATER PARK

2601 S Adams St., Marion
(765) 668-1794
cityofmarion.in.gov

Just an hour from Indianapolis, Splash House Water Park is well worth the drive, especially if your kids relish the opportunity to splash, slide, and swim. The park features a lazy river, a large children's play area with water slides, and one of the biggest wave pools in the state. During special "Power Hour" sessions, the wave pool cranks up the intensity and is limited to bigger kids and adults. Kids can spend the day racing down the twin slides or taking on the swirling adventure of the Big Flush.

For younger kids under 48 inches tall, there's a separate water playground with gentle sprinklers, spraying jets, a dumping bucket, and a shallow, zero-depth entry pool perfect for safe play. Seating is limited, but families can spread out on the grassy areas nearby.

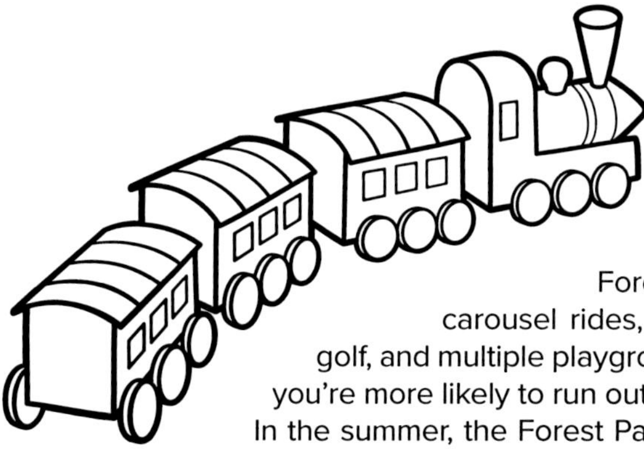

FOREST PARK AQUATIC CENTER

1077 Cicero Rd., Noblesville
forestparkpool.org

Forest Park is packed with fun: carousel rides, real train excursions, miniature golf, and multiple playgrounds. With 150 acres to explore, you're more likely to run out of time than things to do.

In the summer, the Forest Park Aquatic Center is the perfect place to cool off. Families can make it part of a full day at the park or visit just for the water fun. Forest Park Aquatic Center has a 10-lane, 50-meter Olympic-size pool with a waterslide, a separate diving pool with both 1-meter and 3-meter springboards, and a zero-depth entry pool with a toddler-friendly playscape.

Lounge chairs and picnic tables are available, but they fill up fast—consider bringing your own just in case. Discounted admission is offered after 5 p.m.

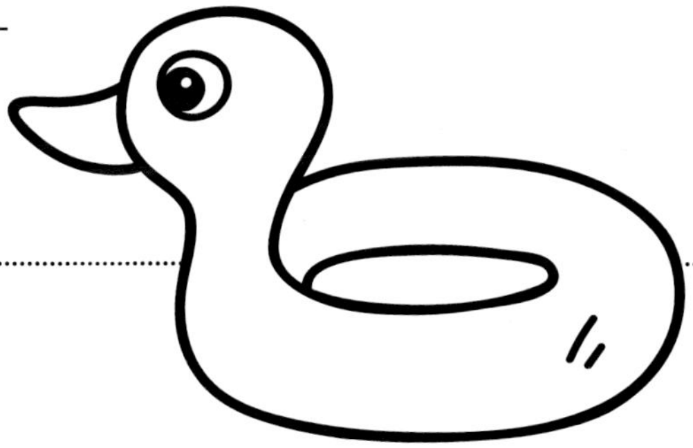

MURPHY AQUATIC PARK

753 S County Rd. 625 E, Avon
washingtontwpparks.org

Murphy Aquatic Park is home to the largest wave pool in Central Indiana, but that's just the beginning. You'll also find two towering water slides, basketball hoops in the pool, and a large water playground with nearly 50 splash-and-play elements.

The inclusive playground features wide, wheelchair-accessible ramps, and water wheelchairs are available to borrow. Little ones can play in their own separate toddler splash zone.

Grab a snack at the Compass Café or snag a shady spot under a sun sail. Lounge chairs are first come, first served, or you can bring your own or rent a cabana to guarantee comfort all day long.

Best Indoor Swimming Pool

BIG SPLASH ADVENTURE INDOOR WATER PARK & RESORT

8505 W State Rd. 56, French Lick
(877) 936-3866
bigsplashadventure.com

Looking for a family getaway that's close to home but packed with fun? Big Splash Adventure in French Lick is the perfect pick. The 40,000-square-foot indoor waterpark means year-round fun with water slides, a lazy river, a water obstacle course, and a children's play zone. In the warmer months, there's an outdoor pool.

The resort also has kid-friendly dining, mini-golf, laser tag, and an arcade, plenty to keep everyone busy.

Some resort packages include admission to Wilstem Wildlife Park, where families can meet elephants, giraffes, and kangaroos. Watch feedings, chat with keepers, or even help out a bit. The seasonal drive-thru safari is a must; you can see more than 40 animal species from your car.

40,000-square-foot indoor waterpark

KRANNERT PARK FAMILY CENTER

605 S High School Rd., Indianapolis
(317) 327-7375
parks.indy.gov

The Krannert Park Aquatic Center is a newly renovated, year-round indoor pool with two swimming areas. One features zero-depth entry and a small slide for tiny swimmers, while the other has lap lanes and a water vortex twist slide that's just the right size for bigger kids.

Admission is budget-friendly. Check the website for open swim hours and Family Splash Time. In the warmer months, the large roll-up doors open to connect with the outdoor splash pad for even more fun.

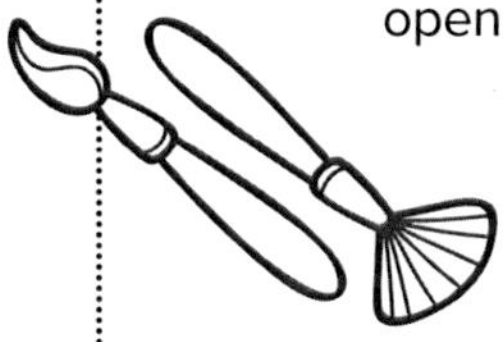

Krannert Park Family Center also offers free activities for kids year-round, like tot playtime, beginning ballet, and art classes.

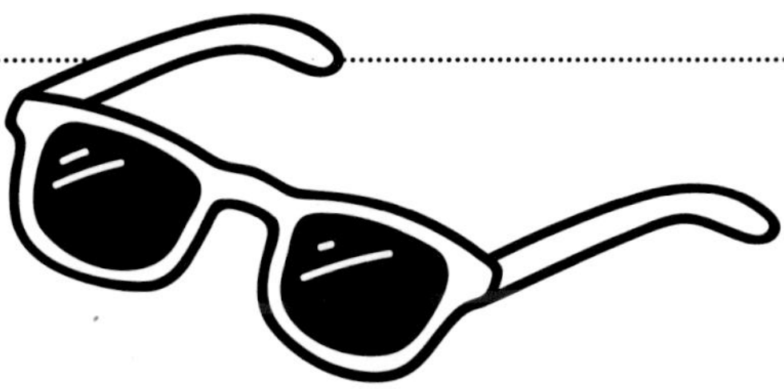

INDY ISLAND AQUATIC CENTER

8575 E Raymond St., Indianapolis
(317) 862-6876
parks.indy.gov

Indy Island Aquatic Center is a fun and affordable indoor spot for year-round water play, rain or shine. The zero-depth entry pool gradually deepens to just three feet, making it perfect for little ones to splash and explore. There's also a gentle waterfall play area and small slides built just for young swimmers.

For more adventurous kids (48 inches and taller), there's the 15-foot-tall water slide that twists and turns before making a splash in the pool. There's also a separate three-lane lap pool for serious swimmers. While the kids play, adults can take turns supervising and unwind in the adults-only spa area.

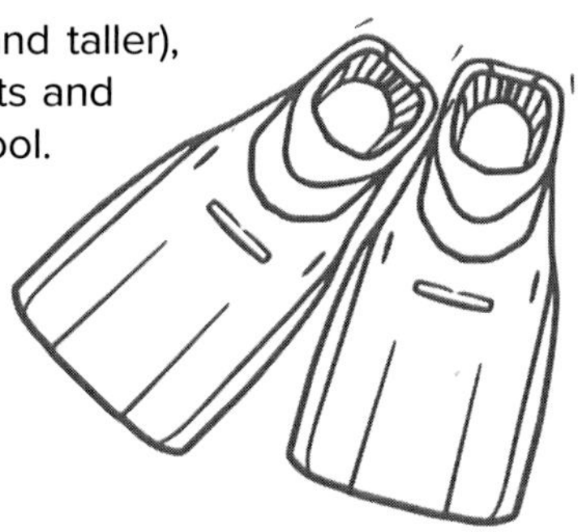

Best Magical Outdoor Celebrations

INDIANA PEONY FESTIVAL

Seminary Park, 350 S 10th St., Noblesville
indianapeonyfestival.com

Budding green thumbs and garden pros all love the Indiana Peony Festival in Noblesville in May. Indiana's state flower is celebrated at this free festival with blooming peony plants and themed items like peony floral arrangements, art, apparel, crafts, and more.

Live music fills the air with joyful sounds, and the festival spreads out beyond Seminary Park along the Peony Trail. Brunch and Bloom is a brunch and retail "crawl" with restaurants, cafés, and shops. Each business along the way joins in the peony fun with special drinks, peony-inspired products, and promos. The alleyways near the courthouse square buzz with live music, comfy spots to sit, yummy food and drinks, and gorgeous floral displays that are totally picture-worthy. And don't forget to vote for your favorite peony window display.

FAERIES, SPRITES & LIGHTS AT MINNETRISTA

1200 N Minnetrista Pkwy., Muncie
minnetrista.net/faeries-sprites-lights

Picture an enchanted setting filled with twinkling lights and children in fairy wings, dashing through the woods in search of magical moments. Faeries, Sprites & Lights at Minnetrista is a multi-day festival that transforms the gardens into a whimsical world of music, dancing, bubbles, storytelling, and crafts.

Kids (and grown-ups!) are invited to dress as fairies, sprites, or woodland creatures. Live performances bring fantastical characters to life, and the bubble garden is always a favorite for little ones. It's a truly magical summer night experience, perfect for making the best family memories.

GREENING OF THE CANAL

Ohio Street Canal Basin, West and Ohio Streets, Indianapolis

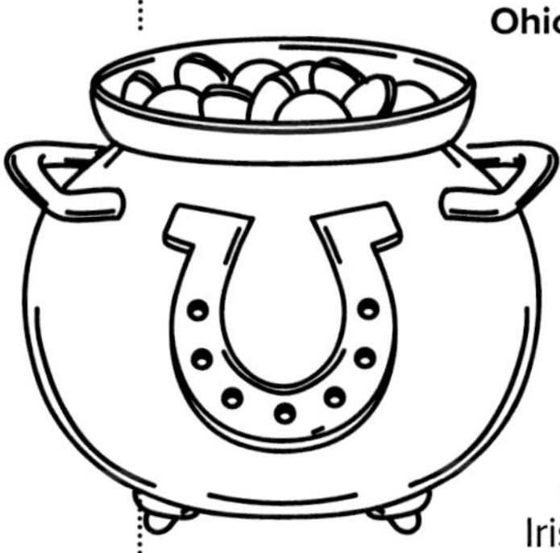

St. Patrick's Day celebrations in Indianapolis are a treasure of festive fun for all ages. There's a family-friendly parade and 5K run, plus the Greening of the Canal to kick it all off. Each year, the downtown canal is dyed a bright green, signaling the start of the city's celebrations.

The Ohio Street Basin becomes the center of activity as crowds gather to watch the transformation. Irish music from groups like the Indianapolis 500 Gordon Pipers adds to the festive mood. Local dignitaries, including the mayor and the Irish Citizen of the Year, help pour the dye into the water, turning the canal green in a matter of minutes and setting the tone for a week of fun.

Best Outdoor Space Like None Other

AVON GARDENS

6259 E County Rd. 91 N, Avon
avongardens.net

Avon Gardens is more than just a garden center; it's a sanctuary bursting with color and beauty. Winding paths and open spaces are filled with blooming perennials, annuals, shrubs, and trees, making it a favorite spot for weddings and afternoon strolls. You'll feel like you stepped into Wonderland.

The garden shop sells plants, gifts, and gardening supplies, while kids are especially drawn to the Fairy Cottage, with its fairy-themed accessories and fairy garden displays. Open April through October, Avon Gardens hosts special events like the Spring-Palooza Peony Festival and Flower Fest, with tours, workshops, and fun activities for kids.

SEVEN PILLARS NATURE PRESERVE

3985 Mississinewa Rd., Peru
acreslandtrust.org

The Seven Pillars are one of Indiana's most awe-inspiring natural wonders. These 25-foot limestone formations have been carved over centuries by wind and water along the Mississinewa River. They're more than just beautiful; the space has cultural importance for the Miami people who historically held council meetings here and still gather nearby. For the best view, head to the south bank.

The surrounding nature preserve has a 1.4-mile trail with a view that changes with the seasons. In late winter, bald eagles are often seen fishing along the river. Come spring, wildflowers bloom across the forest floor, and in the fall, the foliage bursts into autumn color. It's a place where families can go to connect with both nature and history.

MCCORMICK'S CREEK STATE PARK

250 McCormick's Creek Park Rd., Spencer
in.gov/dnr/state-parks

Adventure awaits at Indiana's first state park, McCormick's Creek. Explore a limestone canyon, scenic creek, and waterfalls that are picture-perfect year-round. Stop by the Nature Center for hands-on exhibits and special nature-themed events. The Inn is a great place to spend the night if you want to extend your adventure.

Kids love climbing the fire tower, crossing the stone arch bridge, and venturing into the ever-popular Wolf Cave. History lovers will appreciate the Statehouse Quarry, the source of limestone used to build the Indiana Statehouse. After a day of hiking and exploring, visit the Canyon Inn for a meal and watch for wildlife from the glass-enclosed porch.

Best Place to Explore Nature

NINA MASON PULLIAM ECOLAB

Marian University, 3200 Cold Spring Rd., Indianapolis
marian.edu/nina-mason-pulliam-ecolab

The Nina Mason Pulliam EcoLab at Marian University is a 75-acre natural sanctuary with easy-to-navigate trails that wind through wetlands, forests, a spring-fed lake, and historic stonework. Originally restored using native Indiana plants, it now serves as an outdoor classroom for students and hosts field trips for local schools and scout groups.

Visitors may spot beavers, muskrats, and over 170 bird species. Kids especially enjoy watching the resident beaver colony, looking for their lodge along Jens Jensen Pond. Educational signs along the trail share fun facts about local wildlife and plants. The EcoLab is open daily from dawn to dusk and free for the public to enjoy.

HAGUE ROAD NATURE HAVEN

State Road 38 and Hague Road, Noblesville
noblesvilleparks.org

Hague Road Nature Haven is an under-appreciated 43-acre gem on the north side of Indianapolis, offering peaceful, shaded trails that feel worlds away from the city. Families especially enjoy the Hague Road Nature Walk, an easy 0.8-mile loop that winds through the woods and takes about 15 minutes to complete. Along the way, kids can explore the forest, spot wildlife, and even dip their toes into Cicero Creek. It's a favorite spot for a little creek stomping on warm days.

Though it's mostly natural and undeveloped today, exciting future plans include campsites, a nature-themed playground, botanical gardens, and a nature center. It's already a lovely place for a quiet walk or nature outing, and it's only going to get better.

FRANKLIN URBAN FOREST

Dunn Street, Franklin

The Franklin Urban Forest was created in 2012 by volunteers after a neighborhood was cleared following a flood. This green space near downtown Franklin offers families a chance to learn about environmental stewardship and native Indiana hardwoods.

Along the trail, you'll find a StoryWalk featuring a children's book displayed page by page on signs. It's perfect for little readers. Benches along the path invite visitors to pause and enjoy the growing beauty of this unexpected city forest. As the trees mature, the space continues to blossom into a peaceful retreat. After your walk, visit the nearby city parks and a small art garden just a short drive away.

Best Summer Farm

ANDERSON FLOWER FARM

2284 W County Rd. 300 S, Frankfort
(765) 532-4841
andersonflowerfarm.com

The Anderson family turned their love of gardening into a welcoming u-pick flower farm where families can harvest their own beautiful bouquets. Choose a large bucket (enough for two medium arrangements) or a small one for a single bouquet, and head into the fields. Kids can join in with a mini sand pail, which they get to fill and keep as a souvenir.

There are two blooming garden areas filled with flowers like delphiniums, snapdragons, lilies, and more. Tables are available for arranging your bouquet, and during quiet times, staff may offer helpful tips. For the best picking, visit in the morning (9-11 a.m.) or early evening (5-7 p.m.). Wear closed-toe shoes and bring a container to take your flowers home.

SPENCER FARM

7177 E 161st St., Noblesville
(317) 776-1560
spencerberryfarm.com

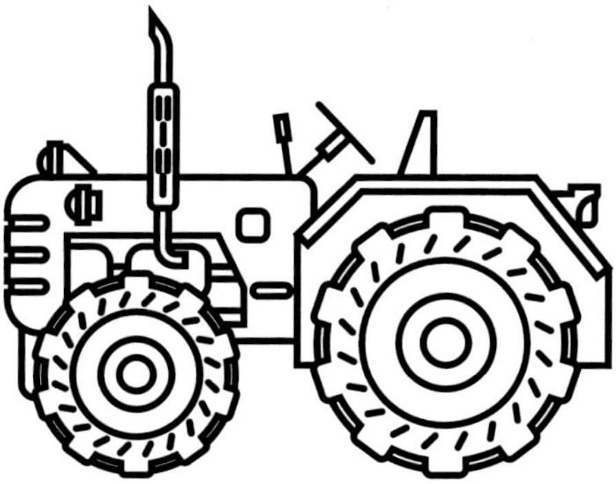

Spencer Farm is a family favorite for seasonal fruit picking and outdoor fun. From juicy strawberries and blueberries in summer to pumpkins and mums in the fall, there's always something in season. Families love wandering the fields, visiting the pumpkin patch, and exploring as the leaves start to turn.

The on-site farm market is filled with fresh produce, local goodies, and tasty baked treats, perfect for taking a piece of the farm home with you. Just steps away, the winery offers a relaxed spot for parents to enjoy live music or play a game of cards with friends and family while soaking in the farm views.

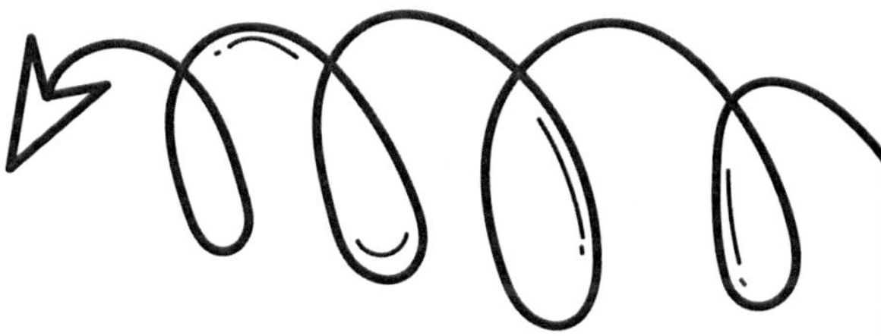

DOLLIE'S FARM

3961 N 425 E, Franklin
(317) 797-7749
dolliesfarm.com

Dollie's Farm is a family-friendly flower and lavender farm, perfect for a relaxing summer outing. Stroll through rows of fragrant lavender, bright sunflowers, and seasonal blooms—all available for picking. Kids can chase butterflies, explore the farm, and craft their own bouquets.

The farm also hosts fun events like bouquet-making workshops and "Pick & Paint" sessions, where guests can paint their freshly picked flowers. "Dollie's Ladies," the farm's friendly chickens, are always a hit with children. Families can relax under the pergola, enjoy a picnic, and browse the farm store stocked with lavender products, honey, and handmade goods.

Best Place for Free Outdoor Adventures

WHITE RIVER STATE PARK

801 W Washington St., Indianapolis
whiteriverstatepark.org

White River State Park is the only urban state park in the US, combining green space, cultural attractions, and outdoor fun. Families can visit popular admission-based museums, but there are also plenty of free activities to enjoy.

Walk or bike the scenic trails along the Central Canal, admire public art, or explore the Growing Places Indy urban farm. Stop by the Urban Wilderness Trail to discover Indianapolis's first Monarch Butterfly Sanctuary, where you might spot beavers, bald eagles, and native flora and fauna. Borrow a bike through the Pacers Bike Share program (Marion County residents get free 30-minute rides) or enjoy a riverside picnic. Don't miss the sculptures along the River Promenade, a peaceful path filled with natural beauty and limestone art.

MIDTOWN PLAZA CARMEL

365 Monon Blvd., Carmel
midtownplazacarmel.com

Nestled between the Carmel Arts & Design District and Carmel City Center, Midtown Plaza is an active community gathering space that hosts events year-round: concerts, festivals, and outdoor movie nights. This urban park is especially popular with families, offering plenty of seating, games, and easy access to local restaurants and cafés.

There's a playground with slides, climbing structures, and interactive musical instruments that keep little ones entertained. Just next to it, you'll find sports courts with shuffleboard, bocce ball, ping pong, and even outdoor billiards. On hot days, kids rejoice in cooling off in the Spray Plaza splash pad. With something for all ages, Midtown Plaza is a great year-round outing for families with kids of any age.

SPARK ON THE CIRCLE

Monument Circle, Indianapolis
circlespark.org

SPARK on the Circle is a pop-up park that turns Monument Circle into a lively, family-friendly gathering space during the summer and other special times throughout the year. It makes downtown feel a little more playful, with lots of room to be entertained, relax, and connect on the soft, faux grass with Adirondack chairs, tables, and shady umbrellas.

Families can play together with oversized games like Jenga, ping pong, and chess. The space often hosts live music, hands-on art activities, and community-building events that bring people of all ages together. Feel free to pack your own snacks or pick up food and drinks from nearby spots to enjoy in this one-of-a-kind downtown park.

Best Place for Wheeled Adventures

PENNSY TRAIL

Greenfield
pennsytrails.org

The Pennsy Trail is a paved walking and biking path built along a former railroad corridor between Indianapolis and Greenfield—though the connection between the two isn't fully continuous. The Greenfield section spans nearly six miles and features scenic stops like the Sister Cities Japanese Gardens, Depot Street Park, and Brandywine Creek—also known as "the old swimmin' hole" made famous by poet James Whitcomb Riley.

Along the trail, historical markers and public art help kids learn about the area's past while enjoying the outdoors. Greenfield also offers a free bike share program for residents, making it even easier for families to explore. With peaceful views and a blend of nature and local culture, the Pennsy Trail is a hidden gem for families who like to walk and bike.

THE MONON TRAIL

Indianapolis to Sheridan, Indiana
bikethemonon.com

The Monon Trail is a 27-mile paved path that stretches from Indianapolis to Sheridan, built along the former Monon Railroad line. It's named after the train that once ran between Louisville and Chicago, and famously carried President Abraham Lincoln's body to Illinois. Today, biking the trail is a favorite outing for active families.

You can hop on or off at many points, with benches, water fountains, and restrooms along the way. Favorite stops include Broad Ripple Village and Carmel's Midtown Plaza, where families can rest, grab a bite, or enjoy some playtime. The trail winds through shaded areas and sunny stretches with scenic views, connecting to other greenways like the Fall Creek Trail and the Central Canal Towpath.

NICKEL PLATE TRAIL

Indianapolis to Noblesville
nickelplatetrail.com

The Nickel Plate Trail is a wide, paved path that connects the communities of Indianapolis, Fishers, and Noblesville along a former railroad corridor. It's perfect for families and riders of all ages, offering a smooth, scenic route for biking, walking, and jogging. Start your journey in Indianapolis near the Indiana State Fairgrounds and follow the path as it winds through quiet suburban neighborhoods, green spaces, and into downtown Noblesville.

Along the way, you'll pass parks, restaurants, and local landmarks, making it easy to turn a ride into a day of adventure. The trail is stroller-friendly, well-maintained, and offers a safe way for families to enjoy the outdoors together.

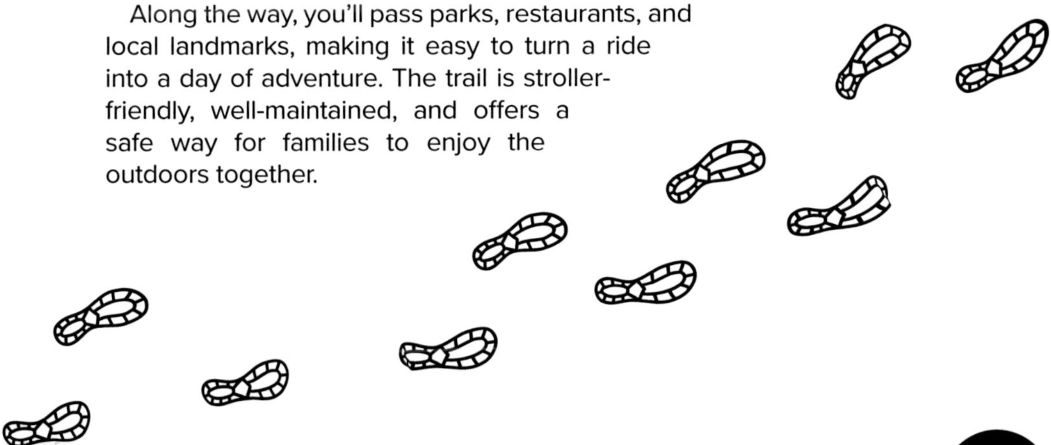

Best Place to Enjoy Summer Concert Sounds

SYMPHONY ON THE PRAIRIE

13400 Allisonville Rd., Fishers
indianapolissymphony.org/visit/sotp

Throughout the summer, the Indianapolis Symphony Orchestra and guest artists perform everything from classical masterpieces to contemporary favorites at Symphony on the Prairie. A beloved Central Indiana tradition, families bring blankets, lawn chairs, and picnics to enjoy live music together in a relaxed, open-air setting.

The casual vibe makes Symphony on the Prairie a favorite among local families who get a kick out of live performances and warm summer evenings. With open seating, guests can spread out close to the stage or near the playground, which is a favorite spot for kids. For those who prefer not to pack a meal, on-site food and beverage vendors offer a variety of tasty options.

DANIEL'S VINEYARD

9061 N 700 W, McCordsville
(317) 248-5222
danielsvineyard.com

Daniel's Vineyard in McCordsville offers a family-friendly atmosphere with live music, karaoke, and plenty of space to spread out. Set against 22 acres of scenic vineyards, the outdoor area features tables, picnic spots, tabletop bonfires, and grassy areas perfect for lawn games, dancing, or just relaxing on a summer night. Along with wine, the menu includes homemade pizzas, fresh salads, and charcuterie plates.

The Summer Concert Series includes ticketed shows geared toward adults, but live music is also available several times a week without an admission fee. A few times each year, the Family Concert Series brings in kids' performers, balloon artists, costume contests, and more. Don't miss seasonal favorites like the holiday breakfast or the grape stomp event.

ROCK THE RUINS

Holliday Park, 6363 Spring Mill Rd., Indianapolis
rocktheruins.com

Holliday Park is a beloved local gem with playgrounds, hiking trails, a nature center, a seasonal ice rink, and year-round educational and recreational programs. Each summer, the Rock the Ruins concert series transforms the park into a venue for live music, set against the dramatic backdrop of the historic stone ruins, gardens, and fountains. This family-friendly event has a mix of renowned and up-and-coming artists across multiple musical genres throughout the season.

Guests are encouraged to bring blankets or lawn chairs and settle in for a relaxed evening under the stars. The ticketed event supports ongoing improvements to the park. While outside food and drinks aren't allowed, food trucks and local beverage vendors are available on-site. Arrive early to find parking, claim your favorite spot, and enjoy time with the community.

Best Spot for Movies Under the Stars

TIBBS DRIVE-IN THEATRE

480 S Tibbs Ave., Indianapolis
tibbsdriveintheatre.com

Tibbs Drive-In, Indianapolis's only drive-in theater, often features family-friendly double features, perfect for a nostalgic and budget-friendly night out. Multiple screens on the property enable the theater to show a variety of films each week. Families arrive early to snag a good spot, let the kids play on the playground, and set up lawn chairs next to their car or pillows and blankets in the car.

Tickets are affordable, children 3 and under get in free, and each screen shows two movies for the price of one. Outside snacks are welcome, or you can visit the on-site concession stand for popcorn, pizza, nachos, ICEEs, and other classic movie treats. Even the family dog can join the fun (as long as they're on a leash).

STARLITE DRIVE-IN

7640 S Old State Rd. 37, Bloomington
(812) 824-2277
starlitebloomington.com

Starlite Drive-In has been entertaining families since 1955. From spring through September, this single-screen drive-in shows double features of first-run movies. It's a pet-friendly spot too, and well-behaved dogs on leashes are welcome to join the fun.

Outside food and drinks are allowed with the purchase of a food permit, but the concession stand also offers all your favorite movie snacks. Audio is broadcast through your car radio, or you can bring a portable radio if you'd rather relax outside your vehicle.

Don't forget the insect repellent, lawn chairs, blankets, and pillows to get cozy with the fam during your night under the stars.

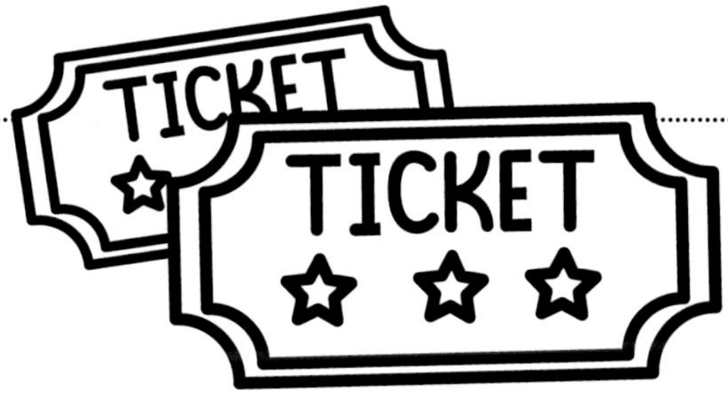

CENTERBROOK DRIVE-IN

6735 State Rd. 67 N, Martinsville
(317) 831-1526
centerbrookdrivein.com

Centerbrook Drive-In, a historic theater, is one of only about 300 or so drive-ins still operating in the US, and one of just four remaining in Central Indiana. It's also the oldest drive-in theater in the Indianapolis metro area. From March through November, Centerbrook shows double features of first-run films, two movies for the price of one.

Families appreciate the spacious grass lawn, perfect for spreading out blankets and setting up lawn chairs. Many visitors bring along games like cornhole, footballs, or Frisbees to enjoy before the show. Kids especially enjoy the outdoor playground and the arcade games inside the concession stand. Pack your insect repellent, a chair, and a blanket and enjoy a fun night out.

Best "Happy Birthday, America" Celebration

DOWNTOWN INDY'S FOURTH FEST

American Legion Mall, Indianapolis
downtownindy.org

Downtown Indy's Fourth Fest is an annual Independence Day celebration featuring a lively street festival and one of the city's most anticipated fireworks displays. Food trucks, ice cream stands, and beverage vendors line St. Clair Street and the American Legion Mall, creating a festive, family-friendly atmosphere. Live music fills the air from the festival stage, while the Kids Zone keeps little ones busy with inflatables and other activities.

The evening wraps up with a dazzling 20-minute fireworks show beginning just after 10 p.m., perfectly synchronized to a patriotic music broadcast on a local radio station. For the best view, head to the Indiana War Memorial Plaza or the American Legion Mall.

GREENWOOD FREEDOM FESTIVAL

Craig Park, Greenwood
greenwood.in.gov

The Greenwood Freedom Festival is a beloved Independence Day celebration held annually on the last Saturday in June. Families can enjoy a full day of live entertainment, activities, and patriotic fun. Kids love the inflatable-filled Kid Zone and the playgrounds scattered throughout the park.

Festivities begin in the afternoon with a lively parade winding through downtown streets, followed by live music and performances on the festival stage. A wide variety of food vendors serve up local favorites and sweet treats. The night ends with a breathtaking fireworks show that lights up the sky and can be seen all across the city. It's one of Greenwood's most anticipated events and a fantastic way for families to kick off the Fourth of July.

SPARK!FISHERS FESTIVAL

Nickel Plate District, Fishers
fishersparks.com

Spark!Fishers is a week-long celebration of Independence Day that brings the community together with family-friendly fun and patriotic spirit. Hosted in the Nickel Plate District, this annual event offers something for everyone. The schedule includes a 5K; an all-abilities one-miler; a car and art show; outdoor concerts; and special nights featuring live music, a drone show, and a fireworks finale set to music.

The highlight is Saturday's Street Festival, where the streets fill with live performances, food and drink vendors, local artists, and shopping. The patriotic parade is a crowd favorite, and kids and teens love the activity zones with games, inflatables, and hands-on fun.

Best Orchard for Apple-Picking Adventures

TUTTLE ORCHARDS

5717 N 300 W, Greenfield
(317) 326-2278
indianapolisorchard.com

During the fall season, Tuttle Orchards is a favorite destination for families looking to go apple-picking. From late August through October, visitors can pick from a variety of apples, including Red Delicious, Ida Red, Golden Delicious, Jonathan, and Cortland. Upon arrival, families select a bag size and head into the orchard to gather ripe apples from the trees. The wide rows make it easy to navigate, even with strollers or wagons.

In addition to apple-picking, Tuttle offers a pumpkin patch, a corn maze, and the FarmYard play area, which features over 30 activities like giant slides and obstacle courses (admission required). Other parts of the orchard are free to explore. The café serves up farm-fresh meals and award-winning apple cider, which can be ordered in slushie form.

BEASLEY'S ORCHARD

2304 E Main St., Danville
(317) 745-4876
beasleys-orchard.com

Family-owned Beasley's Orchard is a favorite fall destination, known for its seasonal activities and fresh, local produce. In autumn, visitors can pick from over 20 apple varieties; take a hayride to the pumpkin patch; and enjoy the corn maze, apple cannons, and Barnyard Bonanza play area with its giant jumping pillow. The Heartland Apple Festival takes place over two weekends in October and features live music, pony rides, puppet shows, and local vendors.

In the summer, families can return to pick strawberries, raspberries, sunflowers, zinnias, and marigolds. Year-round, the farm market, housed inside a restored Civil War-era barn, offers homegrown produce, baked goods, and Beasley's award-winning apple cider.

STUCKEY FARM ORCHARD AND CIDER MILL

19975 Hamilton Boone Rd., Sheridan
(317) 769-4636
stuckeyfarm.com

With 37 varieties of u-pick apples available from late summer through fall, Stuckey Farm is a favorite spot for families to spend a day outdoors. After filling their baskets, kids can burn off energy in the expansive play area, which features the Super Mega Slide, jumping pillows, pedal cars, and a barrel train. On weekends, pig races add even more excitement.

Each fall weekend brings a different themed festival to the farm—Apple Festival, Cider Festival, Pumpkin Festival, and Frontier Festival, just to name a few. To take home a taste of the farm, stop by the Country Market for fresh produce, baked goods, and Stuckey's signature apple-cider donuts.

Best Farm for Pumpkins and Seasonal Fun

LARK RANCH

1611 N Meridian Rd., Greenfield
3145 Killion Mill Rd., Loogootee
(844) 516-6837
larkranch.com

Every fall, Lark Ranch comes to life with carnival rides, farm attractions, and its custom-built, one-third scale diesel train. Designed to resemble a full-size freight train, this scenic ride takes guests of all ages on a loop around the property for a scenic view of the farm. It's a favorite for both kids and adults, and even grandparents.

Little ones enjoy picking pumpkins from the patch, meeting farm animals, and climbing on the play structures. Parents appreciate the chance to enjoy classic fall fun the whole family can share, plus the added value of midway rides. When it's time to refuel, the on-site concession stands offer favorites like pork tenderloins, corn dogs, funnel cakes, and kettle corn.

DULL'S TREE FARM

1765 W Blubaugh Ave., Thorntown
(765) 325-2418
dullstreefarm.com

During the fall, Dull's Tree Farm transforms into the popular Pumpkin Harvest Festival. Families can spend the day exploring the eight-acre corn maze, picking pumpkins straight from the patch, and enjoying more than 35 fun attractions. Kids are especially amused by the giant slides, ropes courses, and barrel train ride. Little ones can climb on the low ropes course, take a hayride, or try the kid-friendly zip line.

Hungry? Grab a bite from the farm's food stands and cool off with an apple cider slushie. You can even rent a private fire pit for a cozy group gathering. Bring up to 30 guests, roast s'mores (kits available for purchase), and make a whole evening of it. Outside food is welcome when you reserve a bonfire space.

PINEY ACRES FARM

1115 E 1000 N, Fortville
(317) 326-1700
pineyacresfarm.com

Piney Acres Farm is a favorite October destination for families looking for fresh air and outdoor fun on the farm. This 73-acre farm has classic fall activities like hayrides; a corn maze; pumpkin picking; and a hands-on play zone with mazes, a jump pad, gem mining, and a playground. Kids can meet friendly barnyard animals, zoom around on pedal carts, or ride the cow barrel train.

The farm store is filled with fall decor, locally made goods, and seasonal treats. When hunger strikes, Piney Pete's Whistle Stop snack bar has you covered with hot sandwiches, donuts, popcorn, and drinks.

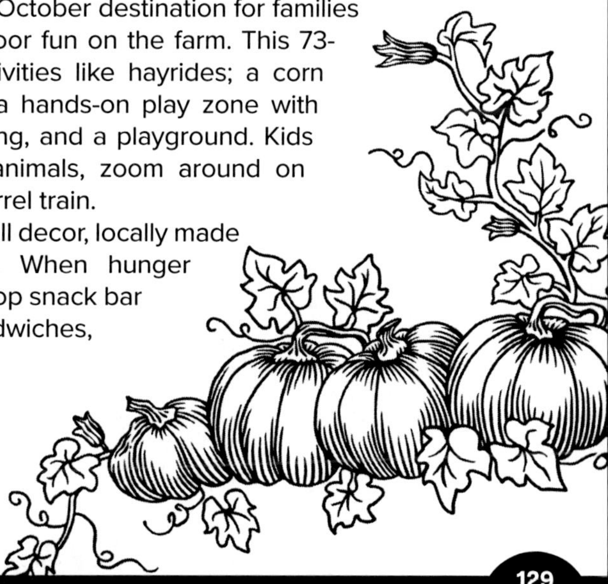

Best Spooky Spot

THE CHILDREN'S MUSEUM GUILD'S HAUNTED HOUSE

3000 N Meridian St., Indianapolis
childrensmuseum.org

The Children's Museum Guild's Haunted House is a longstanding Indianapolis tradition that brings spooky family-friendly fun to the museum. During Friendly Hours, younger children can explore the house with the lights on, cheerful music, and a playful, welcoming vibe. Families looking for more thrills can visit during Frightening Hours, which feature dim lighting, eerie sounds, and unexpected jump scares from costumed characters.

In addition to the Haunted House, there are Halloween-themed events like the Friendly Feast with the Witches, a meal and activities; and Twilight Fright, an outdoor evening event with games and entertainment geared toward older kids and teens. Tickets are sold separately from general museum admission, with discounts available for museum members.

IRVINGTON HALLOWEEN FESTIVAL

Irvington Historic District, Indianapolis
irvingtonhalloween.com

Each year, the Irvington neighborhood comes alive with a full calendar of festive events leading up to Halloween. The week-long celebration includes activities for all ages and wraps up with a Street Fair featuring live music, food vendors, a costume parade, and a Kid Zone packed with games and contests.

Kids get a thrill from the Spooky Organ Concert, a dramatic reading of "The Legend of Sleepy Hollow" in Irving Circle Park, Family Movie Night, and the crowd-favorite Zombie Bike Ride. During the ride, participants dress as the living dead and cruise through the neighborhood as cheering spectators line the streets and wave from their porches.

One of the best parts of the Irvington Halloween Festival is seeing homes transformed with spooky, over-the-top decorations. No one does Halloween in Indy quite like Irvington.

INDY SCREAM PARK

5211 S New Columbus Rd., Anderson
(317) 218-9515
indyscreampark.com

September and October bring serious scares to Central Indiana, and Indy Scream Park is at the heart of the fright-filled fun. Geared toward teens and adults, this haunted attraction offers multiple themed haunts designed to terrify even the bravest thrill-seekers. Each year introduces new themes and chilling additions, keeping the experience frightening.

Your kids won't stop talking about the haunted forest, a spine-tingling walk through the woods full of jump scares and eerie encounters. Another crowd favorite is zombie paintball, where guests board a retrofitted school bus armed with paintball guns and defend themselves by firing at zombies before they reach the bus. Between scares, visit the Monster Midway for food and drinks. Just don't let your guard down; creepy characters roam the grounds, ready to deliver a scare when you least expect it.

Best Place to See Santa

SANTA'S HELICOPTER ARRIVAL AT THE INDIANA STATE MUSEUM

650 W Washington St., Indianapolis
(317) 232-1637
indianamuseum.org

Each year, the Indiana State Museum kicks off the holiday season with Santa's dramatic arrival by helicopter. On the day after Thanksgiving, crowds gather outside the museum as Santa, Mrs. Claus, and a few magical friends make their grand entrance. Elves wave from the rooftop to signal his approach, and families watch as the helicopter circles and lands on the museum lawn.

After touching down, Santa and Mrs. Claus greet the crowd before heading inside for visits with children at the Celebration Crossing exhibit. Additional festivities often include a balloon drop and performances by local youth choirs. Watching Santa's arrival is free; however, museum admission is required for indoor activities and exhibits.

FORTVILLE WINTERFEST

Main Street, Fortville
fortvilleindiana.org

On the first Saturday of December, downtown Fortville transforms into a magical winter wonderland. The day begins with a festive parade winding through the streets, followed by free family-friendly entertainment and seasonal activities for all ages.

Santa is there to hear children's wishes and pose for photos, while the Kids' Zone offers crafts and games. An outdoor ice skating rink adds to the fun. Local choirs and performers fill the air with holiday music, and the evening wraps up with a tree-lighting ceremony. Food vendors serve kid-approved treats like hot chocolate, cookies, and popcorn, and shoppers will find unique gifts and handmade holiday decorations throughout the event.

SANTA'S WONDERLAND AT CABELA'S

13725 Cabela Pkwy., Noblesville
(317) 565-6400
cabelas.com

Each holiday season, Cabela's in Noblesville becomes Santa's Wonderland, an in-store experience with hands-on holiday activities. Kids can explore toy play zones, craft tables, and interactive game stations. Activities often include remote-controlled vehicles, a BB gun range, and practice casting with kid-friendly fishing poles. Children can drop letters into the Santa Mailbox, and if they include a return address, they'll receive a letter back from the big guy himself.

The highlight is a visit with Santa Claus, where families receive a complimentary 4x6 studio-quality photo. Reservations are strongly encouraged to guarantee your spot. The store also hosts giveaways, holiday-themed breakfasts, and special story times with Santa throughout the season.

Best Holiday Attraction at a Museum

JINGLE RAILS: THE GREAT WESTERN ADVENTURE AT THE EITELJORG MUSEUM

500 W Washington St., Indianapolis
(317) 636-9378
eiteljorg.org

Jingle Rails: The Great Western Adventure is the Eiteljorg Museum's much-loved annual holiday exhibit. G-scale model trains travel nearly 1,200 feet of track, weaving through beautifully crafted scenes that showcase landmarks from Indianapolis and the American West. Each display is built from natural materials like bark, twigs, moss, and nuts, bringing places like the Indianapolis Motor Speedway, Grand Canyon, and Golden Gate Bridge to life in miniature.

Families especially enjoy the interactive scavenger hunt, where kids search for hidden items tucked into the displays. With so much detail to explore, it's easy to spend hours watching the trains roll through these magical landscapes. Jingle Rails is included with regular museum admission and is a holiday favorite for all ages.

WINTERFAIRE AT THE CHILDREN'S MUSEUM OF INDIANAPOLIS

3000 N Meridian St., Indianapolis
(317) 334-4000
childrensmuseum.org

The carnival atmosphere and whimsical characters at WinterFaire add to the magic of the season. At the entrance, families are welcomed by Ember the fox, who invites guests into a glowing forest filled with surprises. Children can play carnival-style games, crawl through an ice cave with obstacles, try snowboarding, and discover winter festival traditions from cultures around the world. At the center of WinterFaire is the Frozen Fountain. When visitors gather and touch special metal plates at the same time, the fountain bursts to life with lights and sound.

A favorite for museumgoers of all ages is the Winter Slide, a transformation of the Sunburst Atrium stairs into a slippery slope where kids and adults can race side by side. WinterFaire is included with general admission.

FESTIVAL OF TREES AT THE INDIANA HISTORICAL SOCIETY

450 W Ohio St., Indianapolis
(317) 232-1882
indianahistory.org

The Indiana Historical Society's Festival of Trees transforms the Eugene and Marilyn Glick Indiana History Center into a sparkling winter wonderland. Held annually from mid-November through early January, the event features nearly 100 elaborately decorated trees, each representing individuals, families, and organizations from across Indiana.

Kids get a kick out of searching for the Elf on the Shelf and spotting the Weihnachtsgurken—10 pickle ornaments hidden among the trees. On select evenings, Twilight Nights offer extended hours, enabling guests to experience the trees beautifully illuminated after dark. Visitors can shop for unique holiday gifts at the Basile History Market and enjoy kid-approved treats and drinks at the Stardust Terrace Café. It's a magical holiday tradition for all ages.

Best Holiday Lights

WINTERLIGHTS AT NEWFIELDS

4000 Michigan Rd., Indianapolis
(317) 923-1331
discovernewfields.org

The gardens at Newfields are transformed into a glowing winter wonderland each holiday season. From late November through early January, nearly two million twinkling lights illuminate the campus, creating a magical evening for all ages. Highlights include the Landscape of Light on the Lilly House lawn, where lights dance to music by the Indianapolis Symphony Orchestra, and the Twinkling Trail, filled with giant ornaments and glowing color blossoms. Kids love the excitement of a winter evening outdoors.

Families can warm up at the Culinary Campsite with s'mores kits, gingerbread popcorn, and hot cocoa. Special nights celebrate local organizations and cultural traditions, including Kwanzaa, Las Posadas, and Latkes & Lights. Advance tickets are recommended.

CHRISTMAS AT THE ZOO

1200 W Washington St., Indianapolis
(317) 630-2001
indianapoliszoo.com

Voted one of the 10 Best Zoo Lights Events by *USA Today*, Christmas at the Zoo offers families a festive blend of twinkling lights, holiday cheer, and animal encounters. Throughout the zoo, glowing trees and animal-shaped light displays create a magical winter backdrop.

Children love visiting Santa's Village, to meet Santa Claus, Mrs. Claus, and even Santa's real-life reindeer. Kids especially enjoy a ride on the Endangered Species Carousel, decked out in lights, or a trip on the White River Junction Train. On select evenings, live entertainment adds to the holiday spirit. Christmas at the Zoo is included with regular zoo admission and is a seasonal tradition families return to year after year.

CHRISTMAS NIGHTS OF LIGHTS AT THE INDIANA STATE FAIRGROUNDS

1698 E 42nd St., Indianapolis
(317) 927-7500
christmasnightsoflights.com

Christmas Nights of Lights is a drive-through experience featuring over one million LED lights synchronized to festive music. Families love bundling up with hot cocoa and cookies, tuning in through their car radio, and watching as the lights dance in sync with classic holiday and popular songs. It's a cozy and magical way to celebrate the season without leaving your vehicle.

Highlights include a 180-foot-long, two-story Cosmic Wall of Lights, light tunnels, a field of glowing gumdrop buckets, a Candyland scene, and a massive American flag. Kids especially enjoy searching for elves hidden throughout the displays. While guests must remain in their vehicles, it's still a perfect opportunity to snap memorable photos through open windows or the sunroof.

Best Christmas Tree Farm

DULL'S TREE FARM

1765 W Blubaugh Ave., Thorntown
(765) 325-2418
dullstreefarm.com

A visit to a Christmas tree farm is a wonderful way to slow down during the busy holiday season, enjoy the fresh air, and create lasting family memories. Many families relish the experience so much, they return to Dull's Tree Farm year after year. Kids and adults alike can choose and cut their perfect Christmas tree from over 40 acres of Scotch pine, white pine, and Canaan fir.

Dull's is especially fun for children, with a giant slide, sweet treats, and warm seasonal drinks. On one special weekend, the South Central Newfoundland Club visits, and their friendly working dogs pull trees from the field to the processing area. Dull's is full-service; the staff handle shaking, baling, and loading your tree.

PINEY ACRES FARM

1115 E 1000 N, Fortville
(317) 326-1700
pineyacresfarm.com

Cutting down your own Christmas tree is a tradition that brings families together. From bundling up in cozy layers to wandering through rows of fragrant evergreens, it adds a meaningful, hands-on touch to the season. Kids love searching for "the perfect one," and there's something memorable about choosing, cutting, and bringing home a tree as a family.

At Piney Acres Farm, families can hop on a wagon ride to the tree fields, select their favorite, and let the friendly staff handle loading it onto the wagon and then onto the car. Guests enjoy complimentary hot cocoa and popcorn, visits with farm animals and reindeer, and weekend meet-and-greets with Santa. Trees can also be tagged in advance to beat the holiday rush.

JAY'S TREE FARM

755 E Joppa Rd., Mooresville
(317) 294-0482
jaystreefarm.com

If picking out a Christmas tree feels like just another holiday task, you haven't experienced the joy of an Indiana tree farm. Jay's Tree Farm is a family-owned destination where guests can choose and cut their own tree or select from a variety of pre-cut options, including Scotch pine, white pine, Canaan fir, Douglas fir, and Fraser fir.

The farm offers a full-service experience, including cutting, shaking, wrapping, and loading your tree. Kids love being a part of the selection process and look forward to the special treats available on-site. On select days, families can also enjoy carriage rides, visits with Santa, and delicious offerings from local food trucks.

Best Place to Find Holiday Spirit

L. S. AYRES TEA ROOM

Indana State Museum, 650 W Washington St., Indianapolis
(317) 232-1637
indianamuseum.org

The Indiana State Museum has re-created the iconic L. S. Ayres Tea Room, which operated in downtown Indianapolis from 1905 to 1990. Located on the museum's second floor, the space features original and reproduction furnishings and decor from the beloved department store.

During the holiday season, guests can reserve a table for a buffet lunch that includes signature dishes like chicken velvet soup, tea sandwiches, and miniature desserts. Kids fancy choosing a prize from the legendary treasure chest. On select days, special events like Breakfast with Santa add extra holiday magic. It's a great place to enjoy a special meal and step back in time.

MARTINSVILLE CANDY KITCHEN

46 N Main St., Martinsville
(765) 342-6390
martinsvillecandykitchen.com

Sweet memories are made at the Martinsville Candy Kitchen. Since 1919, they've been making candy by hand year-round, but during the holidays, candy cane production becomes the star attraction. Kids savor watching the magic happen—the stretching, pulling, and twisting of glossy red and white sugar into perfect canes. And nothing beats the taste of a warm, freshly made candy cane.

During demonstrations, families can observe the entire process as the candy is cooked, flavored, colored, and shaped. The full process takes about two and a half hours, so if little ones get restless, you can enjoy a scoop of ice cream in the shop or step out and return to catch different stages of the demonstration.

CIRCLE OF LIGHTS ON MONUMENT CIRCLE

1 Monument Circle, Indianapolis
downtownindy.org

Everyone should take a trip downtown during the Christmas season to see the Circle of Lights on Monument Circle. The main attraction is the Soldiers and Sailors Monument, transformed into a 284-foot-tall Christmas tree adorned with nearly 5,000 lights and 52 strands of garland.

The season kicks off the evening after Thanksgiving with a lighting ceremony featuring live entertainment and the official flipping of the switch—marking the start of the holidays in Indianapolis. Throughout December, special light shows take place, holiday carriage rides depart from the Circle, and families gather to snap photos and soak in the festive display. Leading up to Christmas Day, children can drop letters to Santa in a special on-site mailbox.

Best Place to Step into Christmas Traditions

CARMEL CHRISTKINDLMARKT

10 Carter Green, Carmel
(317) 559-6608
carmelchristkindlmarkt.com

The Carmel Christkindlmarkt is a seasonal event inspired by traditional German holiday markets. The first thing visitors will notice is the 33-foot-tall illuminated Glühwein Pyramid; it's the first of its kind in the United States. Perfect for holiday shopping, the market stalls feature traditional German foods, warm beverages, and handcrafted gifts.

Children and adults can skate on the giant outdoor ice rink and enjoy festive activities throughout the market. The Kinderecke (Kids' Corner) offers free holiday-themed crafts, while the Spielhaus (Playhouse) hosts scheduled family entertainment, including meet-and-greets with Santa Claus, princesses, and fairy tale characters. Don't miss the performances, especially with the Alphorn.

LIVE NATIVITY AT CASTLETON UNITED METHODIST CHURCH

7101 N Shadeland Ave., Indianapolis
(317) 849-2947
castletonumc.org

Each December, Castleton United Methodist Church hosts a live nativity, an immersive event that brings the story of Jesus's birth to life. Instead of reading about it or hearing the story, children get to watch it unfold with real people in costume, live animals, and occasional music or narration.

Guests can either walk or drive through reenacted scenes that follow the journey to Bethlehem, featuring church members portraying key biblical figures. Kids adore seeing the animals—donkeys, sheep, goats, and sometimes even camels. After the outdoor experience, families are invited inside the church's gathering space to warm up with cookies and hot chocolate. It's a meaningful and memorable holiday tradition for all ages.

A MERRY PRAIRIE HOLIDAY AT CONNER PRAIRIE

13400 Allisonville Rd., Fishers
(317) 776-6000
connerprairie.org

Step back in time to celebrate the holidays as they were in the 1800s. At the historic 1836 Prairietown, families explore homes decorated for the season and experience traditional festivities led by costumed interpreters. Kids love interacting with townsfolk while learning about holiday customs of the past.

The William Conner House features a stunning 3D projection mapping show that brings a classic Christmas tale to life. Modern fun includes Kringle's Carousel and the Polar Bear Plunge, a 150-foot tubing hill. In North Pole Village, children meet Trinket Puddingmoon to check the nice list and pose for photos with Santa. Seasonal treats and drinks are available for purchase.

Best Holiday Train Ride

Credit: Visit French Lick West Baden

THE POLAR EXPRESS TRAIN RIDE AT FRENCH LICK SCENIC RAILWAY

8594 W State Rd. 56, French Lick
(800) 74-TRAIN
frenchlickscenicrailway.org

THE POLAR EXPRESS Train Ride at the French Lick Scenic Railway is one of Indiana's most sought-after holiday experiences, with tickets often selling out months in advance. Based on the beloved book, this one-of-a-kind holiday train ride brings the story to life with singing, dancing chefs serving hot chocolate, a live reading of the classic tale, and a meaningful visit from Santa Claus himself, who gifts each child "the first gift of Christmas," a silver sleigh bell, just like in the story.

Families are encouraged to wear pajamas and fully embrace the festive fun. Many visitors turn the experience into a weekend getaway, pairing their train ride with a stay at the French Lick Resort or Big Splash Adventure.

NICKEL PLATE EXPRESS REINDEER EXPRESS

825 Forest Park Dr., Noblesville
(317) 674-3840
nickelplateexpress.com

All aboard! The Reindeer Express departs from Hobbs Station in Forest Park for a 75-minute journey through the scenic countryside of Hamilton County. During the ride, guests are treated to hot chocolate, a holiday cookie, festive music, and visits with Santa and some of his cheerful helpers.

Letters to Santa, coloring sheets, and sing-alongs often add to the merriment along the way. The train operates on select dates from mid-November through December, making it a favorite local seasonal tradition. Families are encouraged to get into the spirit by wearing their favorite Christmas pajamas for this cozy, magical adventure.

SULLIVAN EXPRESS AT SULLIVAN HARDWARE

6955 N Keystone Ave., Indianapolis
(317) 255-9230
sullivanhardware.com

The Sullivan Express at Sullivan Hardware is a holiday train ride experience aboard a trackless train designed to resemble a classic locomotive. Tickets are sold per passenger car, and each one fits up to four adults and two children, making it a great value for larger families, friend groups, or kids who want to bring their grandparents along to visit Santa at the North Pole.

Departing from Central Station inside the store, the train winds through cheerful scenes featuring Santa's elves, reindeer, and even a raccoon band preparing for the season. At the North Pole, children enjoy a relaxed, personal visit with Santa. This event sells out quickly, so grab your tickets when they go on sale in the fall.

Best Holiday Performances

BEEF & BOARDS DINNER THEATRE

9301 Michigan Rd.,
Indianapolis
(317) 872-9664
beefandboards.com

A Beef & Boards Christmas is an annual production at Beef & Boards Dinner Theatre, featuring Santa Claus and a talented cast in a musical filled with favorite holiday songs. Kids are especially delighted by surprise moments, like a flying Rudolph or when Santa shows up. In addition to this revue, the theater typically presents a second holiday show, often a classic like *A Christmas Carol* or *A Christmas Story*.

The all-you-can-eat dinner buffet is a hit with families, offering a wide variety of options including kid-friendly favorites alongside the theater's famous hand-carved roast beef. While children under 3 aren't permitted, discounted tickets are available for ages 3 to 15.

BUTLER ARTS & EVENTS CENTER

4602 Sunset Ave., Indianapolis
(317) 940-6444
butlerartscenter.org

The Butler Arts & Events Center offers a wide range of family-friendly holiday performances for both children and adults. Each year, the Butler Ballet presents *The Nutcracker*, a wonderful seasonal tradition for many families. In addition, the Butler University Chorale and Butler Symphony Orchestra host a free or low-cost concert featuring festive classics.

Past seasons have also included touring productions like *A Charlie Brown Christmas: Live on Stage* and *Elf the Musical*, which bring favorite holiday tales to life on stage. With such a great variety of shows, there's something for every family to enjoy. Don't forget to grab a booster seat (near the theater entrance) to help little ones see better and stay comfortably seated during the show.

A CHRISTMAS CAROL AT INDIANA REPERTORY THEATRE

140 W Washington St., Indianapolis
(317) 635-5277
irtlive.com

Each holiday season, the Indiana Repertory Theatre (IRT) presents Charles Dickens's *A Christmas Carol* in its stunning historic venue, a cornerstone of the Indianapolis theater scene. There's so much for children to look at and see in the building. Families can experience the timeless story of Ebenezer Scrooge's transformation, brought to life with talented actors, period costumes, and an incredible set.

To make the performance accessible to all, the IRT offers both a sensory-friendly show and an ASL/audio-described performance. The production is recommended for children in third grade and older, and the IRT's policy does not permit children under age 4 to attend.

Best Place to Go Ice Skating

MORRIS BICENTENNIAL PLAZA

125 S Pennsylvania St., Indianapolis
gainbridgefieldhouse.com

Right in the heart of downtown Indy and connected to Gainbridge Fieldhouse, Morris Bicentennial Plaza is a public space with multiple activities. You'll find large-scale sculptures, colorful public art, and plenty of places to sit and take it all in. In the warmer months, there's live music, basketball courts, and family-friendly programming. But when winter rolls around? It's all about ice skating.

The Elevance Health Rink opens from late November through late January with 90-minute public skate sessions. Skates are available to rent, and little ones or first-timers can grab a skating aid for extra support. Keep an eye out for special events like free skate days, festive lights, and live music.

THE ICE AT CARTER GREEN

10 Carter Green, Carmel
theiceatcartergreen.com

The Ice at Carter Green adds a bit of winter magic to Carmel with a charming outdoor rink, open from November through February. You can rent skates or bring your own and hit the ice at your own pace. During Christkindlmarkt, the rink truly shines, surrounded by twinkling lights, festive music, and market stalls that make everything feel extra merry.

The fun doesn't stop when the market closes for the season. The ice stays open, giving you more chances to glide, spin, and laugh with your family. Kids will treasure skating under the open sky, and when you're ready for a break, warm up in a heated igloo or around a bonfire with hot cocoa or a sweet treat. It's a winter tradition you'll want to return to year after year.

HOLLIDAY PARK ICE RINK

6363 Spring Mill Rd., Indianapolis
hollidaypark.org

The seasonal ice rink at Holliday Park is open from late November through early March, right next to the Nature Center. Your admission includes skate rental, and if you're new to the ice, skate aids are available to help you glide with confidence. Warm up by one of the bonfires or grab something tasty from on-site food vendors.

In addition to open skate sessions, you can level up your skills with learn-to-skate classes, offered in partnership with the Winter Club of Indianapolis. Occasionally, the rink offers a free Learn to Play Ice Hockey program. Whether you're skating laps or just taking in the winter air, Holliday Park is a fun, family-friendly place to hit the ice.

Best Spot for Icy Fun

KOTEEWI RUN SEASONAL SLOPES

11800 Koteewi Dr., Noblesville
koteewi-adventures.com

There's an exhilarating winter snow tubing experience just north of Indianapolis. Located within Strawtown Koteewi Park, the 700-foot Koteewi Run hill provides thrilling rides down well-maintained lanes. A rope tow system assists riders back to the top, allowing for multiple runs without the exhausting uphill trek.

Children of most ages can enjoy the excitement of speeding down the snowy slopes. The park has snowmaking machines to keep conditions optimal for tubing throughout the season, even when natural snowfall is limited.

Families can warm up in the enclosed porch area equipped with heaters and purchase refreshments like hot chocolate and snacks. Operating hours vary, with extended times during holidays and school breaks. Book your tickets in advance, as sessions fill up quickly.

VEAL'S ICE TREE

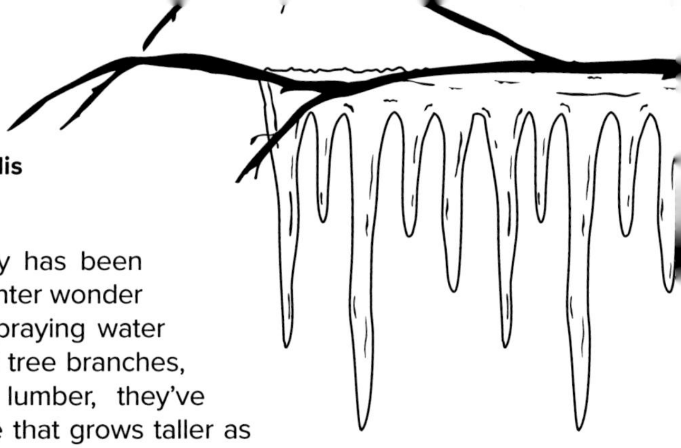

6445 Mimosa Ln., Indianapolis
facebook.com/vealsicetree

Since 1961, the Veal family has been creating a one-of-a-kind winter wonder just off Interstate 74. By spraying water over a handmade frame of tree branches, twine, scrap metal, and lumber, they've crafted a towering Ice Tree that grows taller as the temperatures drop, sometimes reaching over 35 feet! It's like stepping into a real-life winter fairy tale.

Children get a thrill out of magical appearance of the Ice Tree, especially when it's enhanced with colorful dyes and lighting. Visiting the Ice Tree is free, and it's typically at its best during the coldest months of the year. Bundle up and head out to see it. Be sure to park on the designated blacktop areas and enjoy the view safely from those spots.

CURLING ON THE CANAL

Vermont Street Plaza, 414 W Vermont St., Indianapolis
indyculturaltrail.org

You might think about curling only during the Winter Olympics, but in Indianapolis, you can actually try it yourself, no ice skates required! The Indianapolis Cultural Trail has a synthetic ice curling setup each winter, giving you a chance to slide stones and give curling a go.

In partnership with the Circle City Curling Club, the Cultural Trail offers free "Learn to Curl" clinics on select Sundays. Kids are entertained by trying something new, gliding stones across the ice, and getting in on some friendly competition. With hands-on instruction, you'll pick up the basics in no time. Want more practice? Open curling hours throughout the week let your family play at your convenience.

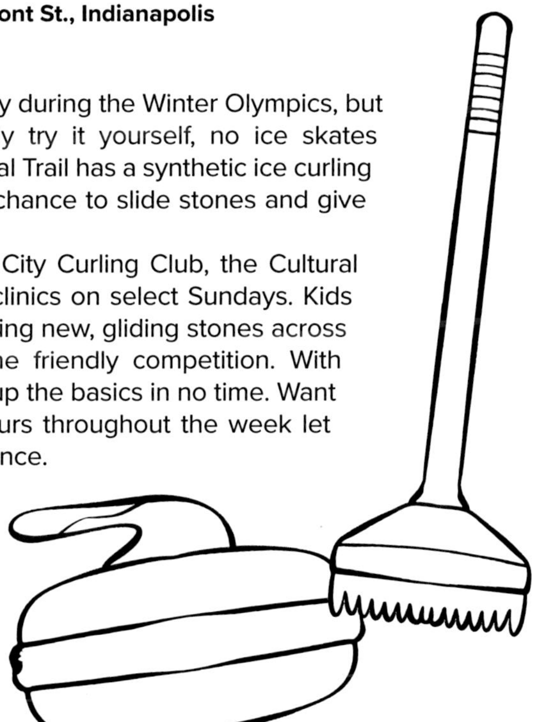

Index